HOW TO
BREAK UP
WITH
ANYONE

Letting Go of Friends, Family,
and Everyone In-Between

JAMYE WAXMAN

SEAL PRESS

Seal Press
A Member of the Perseus Books Group
1700 Fourth Street
Berkeley, California
sealpress.com

Library of Congress Cataloging-in-Publication Data
Waxman, Jamye.
  How to break up with anyone : letting go of friends, family, and everyone in-between / Jamye Waxman.
     pages cm
  ISBN 978-1-58005-597-0 (paperback)
  1. Friendship. 2. Conflict management. 3. Self-actualization (Psychology) I. Title.
  BF575.F66W389 2015
  158.2--dc23
                              2015019613

10 9 8 7 6 5 4 3 2 1

Cover design by Jason Ramirez
Interior design by Domini Dragoone
Printed in the United States of America
Distributed by Publishers Group West

To everyone I have ever been in
a relationship with—then and now

CONTENTS

A Break Up Book
for Anyone

When's the last time you counted how many relationships have ended in your life, and all the ways you let them go?

Odds are, you can't actually count them all. That's because relationships are like orgasms: sometimes they sneak up on you and then suddenly disappear, and other times they last a whole lot longer than that. But when you think about it, no orgasm or relationship lasts forever (spoiler alert: we all die); it's just that some relationships, like orgasms, end sooner than others. The long and the short of it is that you hope to have many of both in your life, which makes it harder to remember them all and easier to remember the best, or the worst ones.

For me, it was only as I began to write this book that I honestly began to explore my own breakups in detail. And, when I reflected back on my past relationships, I realized that I had no idea that many more of them had ended by choice instead of by chance (meaning they were lost in the shuffle of life).

I've done a lot of breaking up. We all have. Whether or not we realize it, this is a common experience. People do just walk in—and out—of our lives. Sometimes they leave with a whimper, and other times it's a lot bigger of a production.

The premise for this book came to me some years ago, after I had gone through a really difficult endship (a term I use for the ending of a close friendship). As I sat there feeling sorry for myself and for my loss (*Or was it her loss?*), I pondered the resources that were available to help me move on. After all, if I could no longer turn to the very friend I was losing, then I needed to find other outlets for my disenfranchised grief.

Sure, there were other people to turn to, but a lot of them were mutual friends who didn't want to be put in the middle (nor should they). Other people didn't understand why ending this friendship was such a big deal. And those who did understand only had limited time, or energy, to deal with a woman mourning the loss of a bestie.

So, I began looking around for other resources. I found that there were a lot of break up books for lost love of the sexy-time kind, but there was nothing out there for a girl who had lost another kind of love—one that was supposed to be guaranteed, like an everlasting gobstopper, to go on and on. It was then that I had this idea that a book about the subject could have helped me feel less alone. Not that a book would always make me feel better or be able to hug the hurt away, but that it could make me understand that this process is something we all process.

We may all do it a little differently, but there are general rules that can help guarantee a smoother and happier ending. And even though we don't all break up, or get over a break up, in the same way, the experience can be similar. That's because there aren't 101 ways to break up, even though there are a myriad of twists on one of the ways you can do it (face-to-face, over the phone/via text, in writing, through a mediator, or by disappearing).

Writing this book also reminded me that there are surefire ways to feel satisfied with a break up. Especially when you have the confidence to be secure, and the ability to stay consistent, in your decision. On top of that, it's important to get clear with your reasons and keep the break up conversation as short and sweet as possible.

Research proves that the gold standard in ending a relationship is face-to-face, and a face-to-face ending provides more personal satisfaction and feelings of closure. I've also talked with people who have ended relationships other ways, for example with parents over an email, by being kicked out of a cult, or with business partners via a text. It's not ideal, but sometimes the ideal situation adds a whole layer of stress that nobody can, or wants to, deal with.

The last two chapters of this book focus on closure and forgiveness. I, along with spiritual advisors and religious leaders, discuss the concept of forgiveness. Yes, it's a complicated word, and an emotional topic. One that can seriously shake the foundation of what you believe when it comes to choosing to forgive someone you'd rather forget.

I have since used this information to have happier and healthier break ups in my own life. I hope my words help empower you to make the choices that work best for you and to speak your mind when things aren't working for you any longer. And whether it's a break up or a break out, I hope this book helps you break free too.

—Jamye Waxman
Santa Cruz Mountains, 2015

ONE

Non-Romantic
Break Ups 101

All sorts of relationships have expiration dates, not just romantic ones. Breaking up isn't always about falling out of love or deciding that this person isn't "the one." Especially since being "the one" and falling in love aren't options in all types of relationships in the first place.

Once it's decided that a relationship with your mother, brother, best friend, cousin, gender identity, church, temple, cult, boss, business partner, acting coach, dentist, trainer, or even your own leg (or any other entity) is not working out, so begins the process known as breaking up.

There are lots of reasons people in non-romantic relationships break up. Sometimes they end because you're not happy or fulfilled. Sometimes they end because being around a certain person makes you go numb. Sometimes you just can't do it anymore, or you don't want to.

You already know the reasons people usually have for breaking up. But when the relationship doesn't involve romantic feelings, it can be way more difficult to explain the break up to anyone—including yourself. Especially when you're still trying to justify your reasons for ending a relationship internally (For example, why did you finally get up the eggs to end the relationship with your sister?), or to explain the break up to other people (How do you tell your mother that you're not talking to your sister any longer?). Most people don't expect you to break up with someone you're not getting horizontal with.

It's also difficult because you're about to end a non-romantic relationship in a world that values new beginnings, or at least multiple second chances. We live in a society happy to "never say goodbye" or, if we have to say goodbye, then we hope to say, "Hello, again," someday. When we refuse to fistpump to the theme song of "Everything is AWESOME!" we may find it takes a lot of convincing (both of ourselves and others) to go with our gut. Still, sticking to our gut is essential, because break ups, while not popular by choice, play an important role in our ability to choose how we live our lives.

The good news is, people are starting to talk openly about their own experiences around non-romantic break ups. Take, for example, the Boston Marathon runner who wrote a break up letter to her amputated leg.[1] Using humor to offset a pretty sucky situation, she showed us that we could laugh about some of the things we have to let go of. Then there was the Philadelphia sex educator who wrote an article about breaking up with her dermatologist.[2] Her letter revealed that sometimes it's not a person but technology that gets in the way. No matter who or what we're breaking up with, we learn there are many other people who have broken up before us.

What Does Breaking Up Mean?

Before we get into the intricacies around breaking up, let's define the actual term. When you think of breaking up, what comes to mind? Is it having to split up various "assets," including friends and family? Or deleting a phone number from your cell? Does it involve blocking someone on your favorite social media site, or pretending the person

TERMS FOR BREAKING UP

Kissing off	Cutting off
Letting go	Coming undone
Disconnecting	Pulling apart
The end	Going our separate ways
New beginnings	A rupture in the force
Unsticking	Disbanding
Separating	Parting company
Splitting up	

never existed? What about voodoo dolls and magic potions—are those a part of breaking up for you?

The definition of breaking up varies, just as the acts around breaking up do. It gets particularly cloudy when the relationship involves breaking up with more than one person or thing, or when it's one person breaking up with their own gender or orientation. In the simplest terms, breaking up is the ending of a relationship.

A positive way of looking at a break up is as an ending that allows you to begin again. Whether it's ending a once-valued relationship that no longer holds the same value or a relationship that's causing you pain, it is the process of letting go. It's a shift in how we think about the boundaries of our relationship, and it's the permission we need to change a relationship that isn't working for us anymore.

Breaking up isn't only the definition of splitting up, it's also a plan put into action. It involves making choices and changes so you can take care of yourself and move forward in your life. It involves learning to build your own invisible fence so that you can protect yourself and set clear boundaries. This figurative "fence" ultimately gives you more freedom and space to move around as you wish.

Breaking up is about taking matters into your own hands and doing what you need to do to feel the best you can feel in a given situation. Ending a relationship forces you to learn to let go, and it teaches you to trust your gut. Once the relationship is dissolved, you can applaud yourself for having the courage to ask for what you want and the confidence to believe you deserve to get it.

Still, breaking up is not a walk in the park. It can take the same emotional toll as deciding to put your pet to sleep. While it's generally a tough decision, there's often a good reason to do it. Often, breaking up can feel scary, and not just because you're removing the bad to make room for more good. It can be scary because change is unpredictable. But change is one of the only constants in life (the others are death and taxes). Like those constants, especially when it comes to breaking up with someone who's breaking us down, we can evade it for a while, but we can't actually avoid it.

Non-Romantic Break Ups Feel Taboo

The first relationships we think of when we hear that someone has just gone through a break up are usually romantic, and generally include going through a divorce, separation, and division of assets and custody. We assume it's about a lover, spouse, girlfriend or boyfriend, a once-beloved snugglepuss, cuddle bunny, babe, or honey. This connotation makes breaking up with anyone else—a friend, family member, therapist, or business partner—feel like a dirty little secret, like it's not supposed to happen and if it does then you've done something wrong. But what if you've actually done something right?

When you think about how often breaking up is referred to in research and in media, you'll find that it almost always involves a "failed" romance. And because break ups have only been talked about in terms of romantic relationships for so long, it can feel like any other type of relationship can't or shouldn't be "broken." It also feels like these non-romantic types of relationships aren't supposed to get to a place where we need to make the ending "official."

Most non-romantic relationships are supposed to come easily, even naturally, or we get out of them easily and naturally. If we have to

FROM FREEDOM TO FAILURE

I asked my "friends" on Facebook to share their thoughts throughout the book. Here they share their own definitions of breaking up. Here's what breaking up means to them:

"'Breaking up' usually means 'goodbye.'"

"Divestment."

"Anything from rejection to feeling insecure, denial, and fearful. Depending on the specifics of the relationship."

"An ending to something foundational, clearly. A monumental change that cannot be denied."

"Freedom."

"Usually one person feels absolutely sick while the other feels hideous guilt. Rarely is it mutual . . . and even when it is it's still usually horribly painful."

"Strike three."

"It's a mixed bag of feelings, including relief, unrealness and disassociation. It's also a sense of self-care, self-preservation, and self-determination."

"Giving up."

"Break ups should be a mutual decision to end a relationship because it is no longer mutually acceptable. They don't need to be angry, sad, or upsetting. We are adults. Getting dumped or dumping someone is not the same, it is not mutual and there are often really hard feelings there. Break ups are okay, dumping/being dumped sucks . . . both are necessary."

➜

"Growth."

"Dissolving a partnership. Can apply to a romantic relationship or marriage. Can also apply to business relationship. Not always sad! Can be very positive. People grow and move in different directions. Life is change."

"Failure."

"That fine line between freedom and pain."

"It is the realization of our ultimate fear, that of being alone (or unlovable). There is a hopeless and helpless feeling that goes along with the realization."

"It depends on how I feel about the person. It can either mean heartbroken or sweet, sweet freedom."

"It's the loss of all the dreams and 'plans' you had when you were with that person. Not always the loss of the person, but the loss of the 'idea' of who you were in relation to that person."

"Neil Sedaka."

break up with someone who we aren't swapping spit with, we may beat ourselves up for not making it work. We may think we're being selfish because a "true" friend is supposed to be selfless. And because they aren't penetrating our orifices, we sometimes fear how the situation will look to those looking in.

That's because when we begin these relationships, we don't think that they will end. When we first start dating someone, we wonder if it will last, or if that person is the one. We check in with ourselves and gauge our level of interest as things progress. We don't usually begin these "other" relationships by Google stalking or getting drawn into the lives of our non-romantic buddies. We don't obsessively text, call, and refresh for new updates from them on Facebook. So, when these non-romantic relationships are working, we don't think about a possible expiration date. But when they don't work, things can get uncomfortable. And because we don't wonder if we're always on their mind—it feels a little awkward when we have to intentionally get them off our minds too.

It's different when a relationship is romantic. Then, we meet someone and (hopefully) slowly introduce them into our world. They, in turn, bring us into their world. Meeting their friends and family is a big deal because they are *their* friends and family—not ours.

During the time we date them, our worlds begin to collide and, if the relationship lasts long enough, some of their friends become our friends too, and vice versa. When it's over, the people we weren't friends with aren't around anymore, and those we did become friends with can (hopefully) easily separate us from our ex. After all, we came from different worlds in the beginning, and we go back to different places in the end. So, we can feel free to share our break up with *our* social circle—the social circle we had before our ex-boyfriend or girlfriend ever came into the picture.

However, you may share a social circle with the person you're breaking up with in a non-romantic relationship. That makes both ending the relationship and talking about how you feel about it being over a really challenging experience. When your best friend becomes your business partner and then the two of you break up, or you stop talking to your mother but remain close with your sister, the whole removal process gets messy.

Because non-romantic break ups are way less talked about, you may not know where to turn to talk about what's happening, especially when it's not just "someone." It may be your family member, a business partner, or a best friend. But a break up with a community, career, or a religion can feel really isolating too. So can a break up with your former self.

On top of all that, there's talking about the reasons we're ending these relationships. In long-term romantic relationships, someone may do something wrong that puts the kibosh on the union. They may cheat, lie, have a hard time saying "I love you," or refuse to introduce you to their family. Perhaps you just don't see yourself with them any longer. In most romantic instances, you can come up with obvious reasons why you're breaking up with someone.

Even if your best friend lied, or your mother was a cold-hearted bitch, having to explain these things to another human being is more difficult than having to explain how an ex-boyfriend or girlfriend did something that took you over the edge.[3] Because a lot of the time, when it comes to non-romantic relationships, the attachments are still there, even if we aren't attaching to them anymore.

What if you're relieved to end a relationship because it was flat and unfulfilling? How do you handle that explanation? While it's sort of like falling out of love, in that sometimes it just happens, that's not exactly what happened. And still, saying "I fell out of love" feels more justified than saying "the relationship was boring." That sounds like you didn't try hard enough to make it work.

There are also common experiences people have after a break up with a lover. We know that in romantic break ups, our heart is oftentimes "broken." You don't have to explain that to anyone—it's a given. But what breaks for you when you end another type of relationship? And what do you call the experience of your sadness and loss? In therapeutic terms, it can be called disenfranchised grief[4]—a term used for the grief experienced when we mourn losses that aren't seen as acceptable in society (like the loss of your stepdaughter in a divorce or a best friend in a break up).

Once it's over, feelings take time to subside and thoughts take time to process. Physically, you may feel that pit in your stomach or that ache in your heart. Psychologically, you have to deal with the loss of a person, or thing, who may still be very much alive but no longer a part of your life.

Whether or not there is a specific reason to end the relationship, other people (be it your family, friends, or spouse) may not understand why you're making such a big deal over ending a non-romantic union. And that can make talking about the end of the relationship feel more like a high-drama mini-series than a way for you to cope with your decision.

When it comes to non-romantic relationships, there's no rulebook on how to get your swagger back. With a romantic break up, you get tons of advice—"The best way to get over someone is to get under someone else," go out, or hang out with your girlfriends—but non-romantic break ups don't always have the same support system in place. If you end it with your mom, you may not be able to turn to your family for support. If you end it with your bestie, you may not find support from your other friends. While support systems will shift, a non-romantic break up can feel lonelier and more isolating because you're not sure where to turn, especially when you just ended things with the only community you've had.

Plus, these people don't get replaced, not in the same way your ex can. Yes, some people adopt a new "parent" when their parent sucks, but in general, when you find a new best friend, there's a different bond, one that isn't exactly the same as your last best friend. And yeah, romantic partners aren't exactly the same either, but you are going to do a lot of the same things with them—like date, have sex, and cuddle.

Even if it doesn't quite feel "right" to end a relationship with the other people in your life, breaking up doesn't have to feel taboo anymore. It's like therapy. Not too long ago, going to a therapist was never talked about. Nobody wanted to admit to going to a "shrink" or any other professional that could help them sort their head out. If you needed head help, you were crazy, right? Wrong. Nowadays, it's cool to have a therapist. And not only is it cool, now there are multiple TV shows about therapy, including HBO's *In Treatment*, VH1's *Couples Therapy with Dr. Jenn*, and Showtime's *Web Therapy*. So, just like therapy is about helping our head, so is breaking up. And breaking up is also about helping our heart (and soul). Maybe someday soon we'll be seeing more TV shows about other kinds of break ups.

Why Does Breaking Up Hurt So Much?

Sigmund Freud, the founding father of psychoanalysis, called suffering an inevitable part of life. But that doesn't make me feel any better about dealing with the pain of a break up. And although I don't feel as alone when I listen to Neil Sedaka sing "Breakin' Up Is Hard to Do," it doesn't make the process any easier.

There's at least one scientific component to all this pain. In 2010, researchers from the University of Amsterdam published a study on the impact of social rejection on the heart.[5] The research, focusing on the functioning of the autonomic nervous system, found there was a measurable, and sizable, response in how the parasympathetic nervous system processes rejection. By measuring beat-by-beat heart rate changes, the researchers found that the sympathetic system (your fight-or-flight, or in some cases fight-flight-freeze, system) took several seconds to get the heart racing. This happened while the parasympathetic system (your conserve-and-preserve response) worked very quickly to slow down your heartbeat. They hypothesized that social rejection and the feelings of hurt that affect the parasympathetic nervous system also play a part in slowing down the timing of the heart beat for a short while.

What that means in terms of break ups is that it actually hurts your heart to go through a break up. That's evidenced in the considerable delay in the return of a normal heartbeat in response to social rejection. And whether you're rejecting or feeling rejected, there's a sense of loss either way.

Isolation and loneliness can increase our stress levels and make us more susceptible to pain. Especially when breaking up with one person means breaking up with other people too. It can feel like losing a part of your identity or your family. If you think of it in terms of losing a limb, you need to learn to operate without a part of you that you may have relied on for your entire life. And without physical therapy (in the case of the limb) or without the resources (in the case of the break up) we need to feel safe and healthy, this whole process is going to take a lot longer to recover from.

In less scientific research, you can't overlook the emotional pain of letting go of the expectations, desires, and plans for the future of a relationship that no longer exits. Breaking up is a loss of dreams and plans. Whether it's no longer spending holidays together, discarding a particular pronoun to describe your identity, or leaving the office or community you helped build up, it hurts to let go of the dreams and ideas of what you thought it would be like. While it helps to embrace where you are, it can be painful to get to that place.

Sometimes breaking up can make you masochistic, like when you spend a lot of time beating yourself up about the break up. You may second-guess your actions. You may question your decisions. These things can take an incredible toll on your self-esteem. If you are the one doing the breaking up, you may be embarrassed or annoyed that you stayed in the relationship as long as you did. Or you may wonder if you were too harsh, or impulsive, in your decision to end things.

Then there's the matter of feeling dependent. We are all dependent on others. This dependency starts at birth, and it's not always unhealthy. In fact, it's a natural, normal way of experiencing other people. Still, when we break up with someone, we have to learn to undo some level of dependence. When people are intertwined in our lives, we have to find a way to delicately remove ourselves from their web. And sometimes, when our history goes back pretty far, getting out of the mess can take a lot of time and preparation. You bring them into your inner circle of family and friends, and then one day they aren't there anymore.

With all this pain, there is some pleasure. It does get easier, and you (most likely) will feel better. Plus, you are giving yourself a huge gift— growth. You are making this choice for a reason, and you're finally taking action to move forward. Don't look back. Change is in our nature, and change doesn't have to feel bad. In fact, you may both agree that ending things is the way to go, making the whole process amicable.

Still, if it's taking more time than you want it to take, you can always talk to a therapist (remember, that's not taboo any longer). As famous German philosopher Friedrich Nietzsche once said: "That which does not kill us makes us stronger." Or, if it doesn't make us stronger, it teaches us that we can survive.

❝ *As humans we mourn the loss of things, good or bad. But when we 'lose' or let go of what zaps our energy and depletes our emotional reservoir, we become empowered to fill the void with better-feeling experiences and relationships. In this lifetime, we have only but one task: to choose. The choice isn't between staying in a relationship or breaking it off. It's deeper than that. It's choosing between clinging or letting go.* **❞**

—Yvette Bowlin, aka The Declutterist

Break Ups Aren't Always Forever

Some relationships end and then begin again. In a number of non-romantic relationships (especially ones with family and close friends), you can reconcile. I reconciled with my best friend *and* my sister. And while we got back together after time apart, the break ups helped us to alter the relationships. We'll explore this further in Chapter Four, but for now, rest assured knowing that even in romantic relationships, 50 percent of young couples try again.[6]

That's because sometimes it's easier to find the common ground needed to work it out after you shake up the foundation. It can be easier than in a romantic relationship because there's usually no sex involved in these relationships (of course friends or business partners may slip up). And without sex, it can be less complicated when you're trying to overcome some of the emotional baggage, making it easier to pave the path to a new place in your relationship.

Breaking Up Is Taking Care of You

You may not be ready to shout it out loud, but say it with me: in the words of Twisted Sister, "We're not going to take it anymore." And by not taking it anymore, you have made the decision to change your life and put your needs first. You're putting your big girl panties on and communicating with the people in your life about what is, and isn't, working. That's all part of the process.

Even if you're just in the beginning stages of thinking about breaking up with someone, it gets better—although it does take time. And if you're reading this right after being broken up with, I know that may not make you feel better. But down the road, you'll know it's true. A break up is a shake up. It's a relationship earthquake, and when things get rocked, it takes time to rebuild, but eventually you do. Your foundation is still there, even if the rest of your world feels like it's in a million little pieces. And while it doesn't get better overnight—sometimes it takes weeks, months, or maybe years—one day, possibly when you least expect it, you'll feel good about doing what you felt needed to be done. You'll feel stronger because you gave yourself permission to grieve. You will thank yourself for being able to break it off, when there may have been easier options.

In the next chapter, we'll get into the ins and outs of breaking up. But, however you go about the process, there are ways to help you take care of you right now. You can exercise, eat a tub of ice cream (which may make you feel bad later on, but sometimes you have to live in the moment), make lists of things that make you feel good, take a trip, get a massage, cry, dance, dive into your work, go out—whatever it is that makes you feel and deal is a good way to take care of you.

While there's been a lot of talk about the sad and hard parts of breaking up, it's also healthy to remember that breaking up can feel amazing, especially once you break on through to the other side.

CONSIDERATIONS FOR THE BROKEN UP

1. Odds are, the person breaking up with you cares a lot about you. In fact, they've probably been trying to care a little less. So before you try to dismiss their hurt, push all the blame onto them, or start begging for forgiveness, take a step back and enjoy some space.

2. Although you may not choose the break up, you have a choice in how you deal with the break up.

3. In order to figure out how this break up impacts you, make a list of feelings, thoughts, hopes, and fears so you can have a clearer picture of what you're dealing with.

4. Find compassion in the process. Have you ever been the one doing the breaking up? If yes, allow yourself to remember what it's like to be on the other end too.

5. Accept that you may never have all the answers.

6. Look at this break up as a chance for more personal growth.

TWO

The Ins and Outs of Breaking Up

*❝ Although you may not always be able to avoid difficult situations, ·
you can modify the extent to which you can suffer by how you
choose to respond to the situation.❞*
—DALAI LAMA XIV, FROM THE BOOK *THE ART OF HAPPINESS*

You're not bad for wanting to end a relationship, but sometimes relationships end badly. And even if you go out of your way to save the day while you save yourself, you can't always avoid an unhappy ending. But you can still try for a happy ending, just not in the massage-parlor sort of way.

I've said it before, and I'll say it again: No matter how you go about planning the break up, no two break ups are created equally. The way one person breaks it off with a bestie isn't going to be the way you break it off with *your* bestie. The way one family handles a change in gender identity isn't going to be the way *your* family handles the change. No two people are the same, so the way one person handles a break up is not the way somebody else will go through the process. And even though all break ups are like tiny snowflakes—unique in all their minute details—all snowflakes are still made of snow, just like all break ups are an act that puts an end to a relationship.

In order to curtail dissatisfaction in the resolution of the relationship, there are some things you can do to minimize the potential emotional harm. For example, in order to avoid an unfinished conversation that leaves you questioning, "Did I just end this relationship?" make sure you are extremely clear in your communication when ending the relationship. Say something like, "This is our last conversation. I don't want to be in this relationship any longer, and after we speak right now, we will not be talking again." Or in order to avoid a dramatic fight, you can first write a letter or text and agree to meet only after the recipient understands the terms of the meeting. And you can avoid a circular argument that ends in frustration around the inability to actually listen or hear one another by sticking to your key points and placing a time limit on your final meeting.

It always helps to be as fair and honest in your feelings (both with yourself and the other party) as you can be. Along those same lines, be thoughtful with your choice of words. Keep in mind that "the best laid plans of mice and men often go awry,"[1] but also remember that you can't have a backup plan without an initial plan. And whether or not the break up happens the way you intended, you should always go into a break up with confidence and the best of intentions.

Break Ups Shouldn't Be Spontaneous

It's almost never a good idea to break up out of thin air. Blurting out your breaking up words in the midst of an emotional fight, for example, isn't a sensitive or productive way to end things. Nor is threatening a break up every time your best friend mentions something you don't want to talk about. And using breaking up as an incentive to get things to happen your way, that's not cool either.

In most cases, ending a relationship doesn't happen in an instant (even if it feels like it does). It usually takes a whole lot of time and a good deal of thought. Even what you think of as a "spontaneous" break up has often been brewing for quite a while.

There are lots of good reasons that a break up should not be spontaneous. Especially since a spontaneous break up will, more often than not, lead you right back to the relationship—problems and all. That's because a spontaneous break up hasn't been well thought out, and if the person being broken up with pleads and promises to change, you're more likely to cave in. After all, it is easier to go back to the way things were than to pave a new way for them to be.

If you haven't figured out your exit strategy, or if you don't have a support structure in place, you will likely fall into your own never-ending story. For a moment, this "fake up" (fake break up) may make you feel like you're being heard, or that you've accomplished something big. But ultimately the other party will call your bluff. They'll return to the way the relationship was, and you will have to either go through this all over again or live with the consequences.

Without thinking through the break up, you're less likely to feel good and stand strong in your decision. It may even leave you looking bad. You might doubt yourself after it's done. It may be because your own brain can't completely comprehend what just happened. Or people around you are questioning your actions. Constant questions—whether your own, or from other people—can drive a person mad.

If your friend or business partner didn't see it coming, a spontaneous break up could leave them shattered too. They may be so stunned or hurt that they try to ruin your reputation. They could talk badly about how you handled the situation, or didn't handle it. And unless your purpose is to really hurt the person you're breaking up with, letting them in on your unhappiness beforehand is the mature way of dealing with things.

With all that being said, once in a while, a necessary spontaneous break up does happen. But that's often because you need to get out NOW. That means you're in a dire situation, possibly with an abusive partner. Whether it's your best friend who has threatened to hurt you with a knife or your business partner taking a hammer to the walls of your office, if immediate harm is coming your way, it's time to end the relationship. Otherwise, take the long way home and figure out how you're going to break up—not fake up or make up.

Why a Disappearing Act Isn't Cool

Along the same lines as the spontaneous break up, you may think about how much easier it would be to end a relationship by going poof in the night. Suddenly refusing to return someone's calls or breaking a standing get-together with no explanation can be tempting. It can be so much easier to pretend someone never existed and try to overlook—or ignore—your situation. It's like when you were a kid and you just covered your eyes, hoping that you were suddenly invisible, or that whatever was bothering you would disappear while you weren't looking. Unfortunately, even if you're not looking, the problem is still there waiting for you. And while disappearing may seem like a foolproof solution to dealing with a break up, because it seems easier than actually having to end the relationship, it's really not.

Sure, you might want to avoid hurting the feelings of someone you once shared a best-friend charm with. Or you're tired of the unavoidable guilt trips that come with wanting to end your relationship with your sister. Maybe you don't want to confront your boss about leaving your job. Whatever the reason, avoidance may seem like the best technique, but technically, it's not a break up if you don't actually go about breaking up. If you just drop off the face of the earth, there's no completion and a whole lot of questions.

It may take some convincing to get you to believe that it's better to cut ties than fade away. After all, making like the wind and blowing toward safer pastures can feel like a clean break, instead of a messy break up. It takes a lot less emotional energy to make like David Copperfield and concoct your own disappearing act than it does to face someone head-on. It sucks to say goodbye. I hate it too. I prefer "see you later." But sometimes, saying goodbye is the best thing you can say.

Besides, while not saying anything seems like the easy way out, it's way harder in the long run. Over time you might feel guilt and shame about the way you ended things, and you'll likely rethink your actions. You may even want to reconnect in the hopes that you can explain yourself, or gauge the temperature for re-upping the relationship (a chance to try the relationship over again). But if you just disappear that first time, then you have no ground to stand on. Because you left in a hurry, the other party might think you don't deserve the chance to slowly work your way back in to their life, especially if it's just to say your piece and leave again.

Not to mention that you look like an ass. You can think you're doing the other person a favor, but you're not. And while making the situation go away without discussion may seem like a kind thing to do to a friend, it's totally cowardly. In fact, the other person has to carry the burden of your refusal to end things with them—at least until they get over it. And they may never get over it, not without closure. So while that doesn't make the face-to-face much easier, never saying goodbye takes a toll on the person you should have said goodbye to. If you want to break up with class, make sure you actually end the relationship.

† ▪ †

Real-Life Break Ups

"I found out a friend broke up with me over Facebook. We were close friends in real life, living in the same city and seeing each other quite regularly. One day when I went to check out what she was doing, I noticed we weren't Facebook friends anymore. She didn't have the decency or courtesy to call and explain what happened.

She just opted out. So, I blocked her. If she couldn't show up to end

things, I didn't want her in my life at all. It's been a few years now,

and I have no idea what she's up to. I still wonder what happened,

and I would have liked to hear what she was thinking, but I'm glad

she's gone. Maybe she wasn't really a friend. I mean do friends

really do that?"

🔒

Research on How We Break Up

When we hear the words "breaking up," we usually think about people falling out of love. Hence, most research on breaking up is based on romantic relationships gone sour. But that doesn't mean this research can't pertain to any relationship; it just reaffirms the need to talk about these other break ups more often.

STUDY ONE: THE LANGUAGE OF SAYING GOODBYE

Dr. Sandra Metts, Professor of Communication at Illinois State University, has done quite a bit of research on the ending of relationships.[2] In one study, she looked at the language people use around disengagement (in laymen's terms, disengagement equals breaking up). Her research found that there were two ways most people discuss a break up. The first was by discussing how their feelings had changed. By changed, the "speaker" meant that either they had diminished feelings about the "the hearer" ("I don't like you as much"), was neutral ("I could care less"), or was disgusted ("I can't stand you anymore").

When feelings weren't the main discussion point, actions were. The speaker wanted to act to undo the relationship contract. By undoing this contract, the speaker was stating a breaking of the rules, in essence ending the relationship. For example, if you watched your best friend's children every Thursday night, you'd no longer be agreeing to watch her children on Thursdays.

Metts found that people generally started the break up talk discussing actions over feelings. That means they'd rather say, "I can no longer spend Thursday nights with your children," than say, "I feel bad when I'm around you." But the former didn't get to the core of the issue as quickly or honestly as the latter did. The research found that if you really want to drive a message home, talking about your feelings holds a lot more weight than talking about your actions.

When it comes to how you break up, what conversation will you have? Will you discuss the end of the business and deal with the details, or will you talk about the way you feel about your business partner and the end of the relationship? When it's not working out anymore with your personal trainer, will you go with how working with them has impacted you, or how you hate Thursday-morning exercise routines? What about when you divorce your sister-in-law? Will you tell her about what she did or how you feel about her?

The answer lies in the type of ending you choose to write for your story. How you hurt and how you heal are up to each individual to decide.

STUDY TWO: AN ATTACHMENT TO BREAKING UP

In the 1950s, Psychologists John Bowlby and Mary Ainsworth developed attachment theory. It's a psychological model that looks at how human beings form relationships. The theory is based on the premise that attachment is formed (or not formed) in infancy at a time when babies have to completely rely on their adult caregivers.

At that integral time in our young lives, one of four attachment styles is set in place. If your upbringing involved a primary caregiver who was there to help you meet most of your needs, you probably developed a secure attachment. If your primary caregiver was inconsistent in his or her ability to be there for you, you may have developed one of two insecure attachments (anxious-resistant or anxious-avoidant). If your caregiver couldn't be there for you, you may have formed a disorganized attachment. Disorganized attachments happen when babies are ignored, abused, neglected, abandoned, or in some other way traumatized. Because people with disorganized attachments have no basis or model for forming attachments later on, they are the hardest type of person to form attachments with at all.

More recently, University of Kansas Psychologists Tara Collins and Omri Gillath set out to uncover how attachment style affects a break up.[3] Their goal was to figure out how attachment played into the ways we break up (there were seven ways of breaking up in their study). They wanted to see if a person's attachment style would reduce negative outcomes—like violence and depression—post break up.

Using various research modalities, Collins and Gillath found that attachment style did impact the level of directness, care, and concern toward "The Recipient" during the break up. It also played a role in determining if a person would avoid a face-to-face break up, or if they would blame themselves for the ending of the relationship.

They found that the more securely attached, in general, "The Disengager" was when ending things, the more likely they were to do so directly, face-to-face, and with compassion. And, they found this direct and compassionate approach reduced the negative post–break up outcomes.

Now think about how you attached to your primary caregiver and how that may have impacted your approach to relationships. Whatever style you may have been born into, how can you handle your break up with the security, authenticity, and awareness of a securely attached person? Can you communicate your feelings about the break up from a real, genuine place and not an angry, resentful one? You can if you use phrases like "This isn't working for me" and "I'm trying to meet my needs." Own your reasons, actions, feelings, and words. Do it face-to-face whenever you can, if for no other reason than out of respect for a dying relationship.

FACT: *Did you know that Neal Sedaka recorded two versions of "Breakin' Up Is Hard to Do?" In 1962 it was upbeat with a lot of doo-wop, and in 1975 it was slow and melancholy.*

Seven Steps to Breaking Up

There isn't a magical formula for how to break up. There aren't a specific number of steps you have to follow to dance the dance of the undoing, but seven is a significant number. And because I like to find significance in everything, including the act of breaking up, seven is a well-thought-through number of steps to take to ensure you're willing to end the relationship. These steps are meant to help prepare you for the break up, making sure that you've taken care of yourself so you can handle any conversation that may come your way. These seven steps are there to help you before, during, and after a break up. They are designed to lay the foundation for a break up conversation that doesn't leave you stammering for words or struggling for strength.

STEP ONE: SET YOUR MIND TO IT

Before you head into the break up, make sure you have every intention of ending the relationship and you understand what it means to no longer have this person in your life. It's really important to be sure you're ready and willing to lose the relationship when you actually do it. If you can't wrap your head around actually ending the relationship, wait until you can, or figure out an alternative plan for living with this person in your life. Don't go back and forth in your decision—it's not good for you or the break up.

If you initiate a break up before you have confidence and clarity, then you can really mess with the person you're breaking up with. They may be unsure where they stand. They may question your intentions, or wonder if you're just having a momentary bout of crazy. On the flipside, they may end things with you before you get to say your piece, especially if you go back and forth in your decision too many times.

If you haven't set your mind to it, you may say things you don't mean. A lot of times we say hurtful things to the person we're breaking up with so we can push them away. Or we push their buttons so we can get them to do the hard work for us. And sometimes we drag

THE SIGNIFICANCE OF SEVEN

Seven is significant in a lot of ways. For the religious set, it's the number of days it took to complete creation. For those who believe that each week is a new beginning, there are seven days in the week. If rainbows are your good-luck charm, then look toward the seven colors in the rainbow. In the Chinese culture, the number seven is a lucky number for relationships. In Western cultures, it also signifies good luck. For literature geeks, seven is considered the most magically powerful number in the Harry Potter series—of which there are seven books. It's also used in Neil Gaiman's *Sandman* series when referencing the 7 Endless—Destiny, Death, Dream, Destruction, Despair, Desire, and Delirium—a group of men and women meant to embody the most powerful forces of the universe.

them back into our thought process. We do this because we're not really sure we can go through with the break up. And it's a lot easier to have someone else initiate the ending for us. It may feel better to wait for someone else to end the relationship, but that's manipulative and exhausting for everyone involved. Slipping back and forth between certainty and indecision can take a toll on your mental and physical health too. Uncertainty can cause depression, anxiety, and paranoia. It can give you a serious case of the blahs and decrease productivity in other parts of your life. So, when it comes to ending a relationship, ask yourself some questions. For example, what feelings come to mind when you think of no longer having this person in your life? Are you sure you can't, or don't want to, work on making the relationship better? Are you willing to never speak to this person again? Who can you turn to for support when you end this relationship?

Be clear about what you're going to lose by ending the relationship.

Be honest with yourself about what's at stake. If you're unclear about what it means to lose the relationship, you'll be less prepared to deal with the loss. And, yes, you can never be fully prepared for what you might lose, but it can help with the recovery if you have some idea of what is not going to be in your life anymore (the good and the bad).

Once you set your mind to it, set the person you're breaking up with free too.

STEP TWO: BE DETAIL ORIENTED

Think about the details required to end the relationship. Make a checklist of things you want to make sure to say during the break up. Things to think about include: Where will you meet? How will you begin the conversation? How long are you willing to stay to hear them out? What are the next steps? How will you end the interaction?

As far as determining the details, while it will vary depending on the relationship, it's best to stick with short and sweet. Set a time limit of no more than sixty minutes, unless it's a relationship that includes a lot of minute details involved in tying up all loose ends. Be specific about setting the time frame beforehand. Give them an exact time you will meet and an exact time you will need to leave by. Even if they are late, leave when you said you would.

Meet in a public place that also allows for some privacy. Try a coffee shop with tables, or a park with lots of benches. When you approach the conversation, you'll want to bring up the most important points, including anything that needs to be taken care of after you've stopped talking. (For example, if you're breaking up with a sibling but you both still have to be involved in your parents healthcare, who handles what? Or if you're breaking up with a friend, perhaps discuss a time frame for when you can both be in the same room with all your other friends.) You may not get all the answers you need that day, but it's okay to bring a list of things you want to make sure you talk about.

Get in touch with what you valued about the relationship, and accept that what was valued will be gone. Also figure out what you were getting out of staying. Did you honestly want the business to work? Were you looking to please your pastor? Did you want to look good to your friends? Figure out ways to replace what you're losing, and remind yourself that you can survive. You will be okay.

Also, instead of thinking about just how different your life will be without this person, career, or community, think about exactly what will be different. Are you losing your financial security? Without this person in your life, will you never know when the next best party is? Will you no longer be able to go to your Aunt Emme's for dinner every other Sunday? Are you giving up on the idea that you'll ever be a Supreme Court Justice by switching careers? Be specific about what has kept you going in the relationship, and be consistent about the reasons the relationship is now tearing you apart.

The more specific and consistent you can be about the mechanics and impact of the break up, the more likely you'll be heard before you end things. And the more likely you'll be able to stay broken up.

STEP THREE: DON'T PLAY THE BLAME GAME

Before you have a conversation about why you're breaking up, it's important to understand your role in the end of the relationship too. As you take responsibility for your role in the break up, don't blame it all on yourself (unless it's actually your fault) or all on the other person. A lot of times we try to assign blame, either to the other person or ourselves, because we feel bad about our decision. We may try to rewrite reality so that we can feel better, or more justified, blaming someone for the break up. Sometimes we try to figure out ways we could have prevented it from happening. But the past has happened, and the future is ours to create.

Stop with the what-ifs and focus on the what's next. Accept yourself. You're not perfect. Neither are they.

Whatever happened has happened. It's time for the relationship to transition. So, like you would for a dying relative, make the end as comfortable as possible. Don't try to sugarcoat the situation, and don't try to make it different than what it was or is. Because when it's over, it's over just the same.

STEP FOUR: YES! YOU! CAN!

Be excited about your rebirth and approach this break up like it's game seven of the World Series, bottom of the ninth, bases loaded, the winning run on third. Go all out with the old and in with the new. Feel strong and confident about taking bold steps. Be excited for the future. Be excited by your strength and determination, and use that excitement to break free. Use this excitement to approach the break up with all you've got. Give the "recipient" your truth. Give them a chance to speak too, and try to leave the conversation feeling excited about a future you have yet to write.

You'll have plenty of time to mourn what is lost, so get pumped up about creating space for new people and activities in your life. Make a list of activities you want to accomplish. Will you start your own business? Join group therapy? Go camping? Find a new meditation practice?

Even if you decide to do nothing but accept that you have lost a parent, friend, business partner, career, or gender identity, think about how you've gained a bit of independence, confidence, and strength by making the decision to move on.

STEP FIVE: DON'T GET TRAPPED

I'm talking physically and emotionally here. Psychologist Michael Tomasello, in his book *Why We Cooperate*, argues that human babies, from fourteen months on, have an innate sense that helping others is beneficial to survival.[4] If that's the case, and we're born believing that we are better off saving than severing, it can be easy to fall into the trap of never letting go. But sometimes you need to let go of someone else so you can save yourself.

Make sure you have clear boundaries once you've put the break up in motion. As relationship coach Marcia Baczynski explained,

"People are willing to take as much as you're willing to give. Especially when there is a prior established intimacy. We all train each other on how close it's okay to be. So resetting those boundaries means telling the other person that it's not okay to come over and hang out like they used to."[5]

That means it's imperative to say no to things that will trap you in the relationship. It's okay to say no to a request for one more chance. It's okay to refuse to meet at a time you're not comfortable meeting. It's okay to refuse to meet in private. Creating and maintaining your boundaries helps give you a sense of freedom. It helps you avoid getting trapped into compromising yourself so the other person hurts less.

Creating boundaries allows you to maintain self-preservation, but you may want to keep a physical exit strategy in mind just in case. Choose the location of your break up discussion wisely. Unless you choose to set your break up date in the La Brea Tar Pits, there are very few places you can get physically stuck in, but that doesn't mean that you can't find yourself in a spot that's hard to get out of. Find a public place with an easy exit. An open space, somewhere outdoors, is always a good choice for not feeling trapped.

STEP SIX: FEEL THE BURN

There's no sense in pretending that you're a statue of serenity when it comes to the break up, whether you're in the planning stages or during the actual conversation. It's okay to feel upset, relieved, or discouraged about your situation. Just because you're making the choice to end things doesn't mean you should hide the fact that you're sad, satisfied, disheartened, nervous, or all of the above. In fact, the more real you can get, the more real the impact of the break up will feel—both in the moment and after.

However, if you think that letting your emotions out is going to make it easier for the other party to take advantage of you, by all means, remain stoic. Being upset and letting them know that this hurts you too is okay, as long as the hurt doesn't hamper the decision or the outcome.

It's okay to cry, to get angry, to laugh at the good times you shared. It's okay to let the person know you care about them, even if it has to be from a distance from this moment on. If you have feelings about the break up, it's all right to feel them.

STEP SEVEN: GET A MANTRA

Okay, you may think mantras are only for praying or meditation, but they're not. And you may think you don't need to repeat something over and over to make yourself get past a break up, but it can really help. A mantra is a word, phrase, or slogan repeated often that expresses your beliefs or feelings.

I have used mantras to get over break ups in my own life. In 2009, I decided to break up with my favorite city in the world, New York, and venture out west to Los Angeles. I felt like I was breaking up with the longest relationship I'd ever had. I'd been in New York for fourteen years, and, when I thought about leaving the city, I felt like I was leaving the love of my life. This was the city that had given me so many great memories and had supported me throughout my twenties and half of my thirties. I was leaving it for a place that I didn't know well, a place without winter, a place where sunshine was plentiful and people were artificially nice. It was a total culture shock. I even remember having a breakdown in a drugstore because the store was too big and I missed my cramped spaces and small aisles.

My sarcasm, my affinity for black leather boots, and my desire to walk everywhere were some of the things being lost in translation. On top of all that, I was doing this alone. I didn't have a job waiting for me when I arrived in Los Angeles. I didn't have a relationship I was moving across the country for. I had a few friends out west but a lot more close friends on the East Coast. And most of my family, with the exception of a few stragglers, was all in the range of New York, New Jersey, and Connecticut. I didn't have a reason to go, but still I went.

I was scared. And every time I felt the fear building up inside of me, I recited a mantra. The mantra I chose was one I had heard from famed oddball and tour guide Timothy "Speed" Levitch. In his book *Speedology*, he writes, "Fear is joy paralyzed." Hearing it in my own voice every time I was afraid of what I was about to do made me stronger and more excited about my move. Those four words provided me with comfort. I believed there would be something wonderful on the other side of my fear.

My mantra reminded me of riding a roller coaster. Heading up to that first steep drop stirred up anticipation, fear, and twisted knots in my stomach. But once I took the plunge, I could breathe freely and even laugh at the thrill of the ride. The mantra always helped me get over the drop and reminded me that the things I was most scared of were holding me back from finding things that brought me joy—the kind of joy captured in the Charles Schultz moments when he drew Snoopy dancing, head high, feet fast.

There are a whole host of other empowering mantras that you can use. You just have to find one that works for you. Think of a favorite book or movie quote or a favorite song lyric. (I think of Destiny's Child's "I'm a Survivor" when I need a boost these days.) Use Maya Angelou's inspirational poem "Still I Rise" or a favorite line from a speech by a fierce leader. For example, Martin Luther King Jr.'s August 1963 "I Have a Dream" speech is a good source of inspiration. Use a mantra from a yoga practice or meditation. Or create your own.

You can create your own by writing out your feelings about the break up and the feelings you expect to have once it is done. Then use one of your own lines to help you get through this. You can also think about how the relationship makes you feel—angry, sad, lonely, small— and find a mantra that refutes that feeling. When you find your mantra, you can leave it here, so every time you need to, you can turn back to this page and say:

(Write your own mantra here.)

_____

_____

_____

_____

Now, doesn't that help you feel stronger?

Baby Steps Still Move You Forward

No matter how you break up, or with whom you break up, we all have to deal with the end of the "us." Whether it's the us of community, the us of friendship, or the us of a former identity, what once was is no more. We have to all deal with the fact that a dream is dead. The break up is the burial. And after it's buried, we have a choice about how we remember the relationship. How long do we mourn? Do we honor and celebrate what was? Or are we remiss about what we didn't get to do before it was gone?

While you may not fall into the sand traps and pitfalls as you walk along the road to break up recovery, they will be there, trying hard to bring you down. After a break up, you may not feel so good. You may immediately decide you made a wrong decision. You may want to erase the last conversation and make the hurt go away. But before you text, call, or show up in the place you just left—take a breath. There's a reason you went through with your plan, so give yourself some time to let it all sink in.

You may find that you start to revise reality. Maybe you decide that you just weren't seeing your sister-in-law's good intentions. Or you start to believe that your friend's demands on all of your time meant she really liked being around you. You start to feel that you're depriving the person you just broke up with of something really important— more time to make it right.

Or maybe you exaggerate your feelings of loss. You may think that losing this person, this job, this identity is affecting every inch of your life. While the end of a relationship has a large impact on our lives in the here and now, we tend to expand the importance of the relationship in the moment. We have to remember that the relationship and subsequent break up aren't the only things that exist in our world.

What you can do in this instance is figure out how you're going to stay busy. Do you find a support group? Join another church? Go to the gym? Take a class? Go on a vacation to get away from your familiar surroundings?

Who can you turn to? Turn to other friends, your partner, a therapist, or a new exercise routine for support. Turn to your journal and get your thoughts down on paper. Turn to school, work, or a new community. Just make sure you have someplace to go, or someone to go to.

There is no right or wrong way to feel after a break up, and only you can decide what types of activities will help you move forward. You may hit a bump, or a larger obstacle, in the road. But once you get past the break up, you will find a new sense of strength and accomplishment.

Look at each moment as just that: a moment in time. A right now, not a forever. How you feel the day after the break up may not reflect how you feel in the weeks, months, and years to come. It is only in this moment that you feel this way. Everything in life is subject to change.

Take a Break from Thinking About the Break Up

You weren't born with a crystal ball attached to your hand, so you can't predict exactly how your break up will play out. You may be wondering how long you'll need to avoid all contact, or how you'll deal with each other when you come into contact again. You may be curious about what other people are saying about the fact that you had the stones to break up with your dad. You may be wondering if you've done the right thing by leaving a high-paying job to start your own business or if you'll ever find a place to practice your new religion.

The best thing you can do for yourself is stop thinking about everyone and everything else. In fact, it would be great if you could stop thinking about the break up at all. Perhaps you can put a moratorium on thinking about the relationship, the what-ifs and the what's next, for a specific period of time—maybe three months. Then you can see how you are after that.

Yeah, that may seem easy for me to say. I'm not in your brain, but I have my own brain. And it does a lot of the same things your brain probably does too. So when I think about something that I don't want to think about any longer, I push a new thought into my brain space. For example, when I start to get down on the end of a friendship, I think about all the great friends I currently have. When you get down about the termination of a dream, think about the new dreams you will create. Go back to your mantra, or blast your favorite song and have a dance-off with yourself. Go to a movie or listen to your favorite podcast. Most importantly, trust yourself to do the right thing in the right time. You'll have plenty of time to figure out your next steps. So don't worry about trying to figure it all out now.

CONSIDERATIONS FOR THE BROKEN UP

1. Remember that breaking up is also hard for the person ending the relationship.
2. A failed relationship does not impact your value as a person.
3. Find a support circle. Don't be afraid to reach out.
4. Old feelings will surface, so it's good to have someone you can talk to, like a therapist or coach.
5. Take time to heal.
6. Avoid bad habits to numb your rejection or your guilt.
7. It's not all your fault. But it doesn't hurt to look at what happened and examine your role in it.

THREE

Relationships Gone Bad

When a relationship stops working, it can begin to feel slightly annoying or outright harmful. Relationships vary in awfulness, ranging from plain old boring to frustrating and, when they're at their worst, toxic. These dysfunctional relationships don't offer us much in terms of, well, anything.

These relationships seem lackluster because they lack luster in every possible respect. This person isn't someone you can lean on when you feel like you're falling. They aren't someone you can turn to when you need an ear. This person doesn't offer much in terms of insight or activity, and yet you have felt obligated to endure the relationship. While these relationships aren't necessarily impacting your ability to function in your life, they may be aggravating and unnecessary. They may be preventing you from moving on to find other, more beneficial relationships. Despite the fact you probably haven't thought much about it, you do have a way out. You can break up with these people.

On the other hand, there are relationships that *need* to end. These are relationships that are actually bad for you. They may be causing you distress and other disturbances in your Force. Generally referred to as toxic relationships, these are the relationships that can be emotionally draining or even abusive.

When you think of the word toxic, what comes to mind? A filthy green glob of stinky garbage? *The Toxic Avenger*, Sloth from *The Goonies*, or some other cult movie monster? Or maybe even actual poison? No matter what image you conjure in your mind, odds are, it's not good.

Healthy relationships generally include mutual respect, admiration, caring, responsibility, and open, honest, and direct communication. Toxic relationships may begin with some of these same qualities, but in the end, they spiral into a hopeless pit of despair, negativity, lack of communication, disrespect, gossip, and other ugly goblins.

When a relationship becomes toxic, it can ruin your life. You may not be able to stop thinking about what's wrong with the relationship, or with you for being *in* the relationship. You may notice limited productivity and a lot more insecurity around your own beliefs. Your self-doubt may skyrocket while your self-worth plunges deep down into the depths of darkness. You will likely learn to compensate for what you've lost by shutting down. Toxic relationships stink, and although these relationships are really bad for us, they can also be the hardest to get out of.

The Bad Rap Around Dependency

If you think back to all you've accomplished, all your best moments and your greatest achievements, odds are, someone else was involved. Someone else may have been there to share in your joys, your sorrows, your successes, or your failures. In fact, you might feel like you couldn't have done what you did, or gotten through what you went through, alone. This dependency on the "kindness of strangers" or the help of those closest to you is something that has allowed you to work on yourself and your life. Let's face the music: we all get by with a little help from our friends.

However, relationships built on codependency or counter-dependency can quickly go south. That's because these two types of dependence are defined by an unequal power dynamic.

Codependency is a term used to describe relationships where the balance of power is explicitly in the hands of one person.[1] These relationships don't allow the other person to be who they actually are. The term originally referred to relationships with alcoholics, but it can happen in any relationship—whether the person drinks or not.

Counter-dependency is basically the classic teenager move, when a young adult wants nothing more than to be everything her parents aren't. It's the "I don't need anyone" attitude. It happens a lot in relationships where we feel so alone that we don't want the help of others. Signs of counter-dependency can include the need to always be right, or to stay away from everyone else so you don't feel wrong.[2] From the outside, it looks like trying to assert independence, but it's actually more of an attitude of fear of being hurt or let down.

When dependency is balanced well, it's called interdependency. Interdependency is the sense that we all rely on one another, but not too much, to keep on keeping on.[3] It is the healthiest type of dependency to have in any relationship.

Learning to Say No

No is a small word with a big punch. It's not only an important word to practice while in a relationship; it's also an essential word to know how to use when ending a relationship. That doesn't make it an easy word to use, especially when we grow up learning that *no* is a bad word only used when we do bad things.

It's hard to undo what you may have learned about saying no. You may say yes out of guilt, or because you have our own inner conflict about letting someone down. You may believe you can make things right by not "running away" with a hasty no. But saying no isn't about running from something; it's about staying in your power and standing your ground.

Saying no can be challenging, but when you think of the benefits—less stress, more opportunity, personal growth, development, and self-care—it's worth learning how to use this little, big word. We need to be able to say no in order to have more room for yes. While that may seem like a contradiction in terms, no is really a way to open the door for a big yes!

> **❝** Part of the reason I'm so big on the no is that it creates space for honest yeses. And if you can't honestly be a no, then you're being coerced into a yes. **❞**
> —MARCIA BACZYNSKI, WWW.ASKINGFORWHATYOUWANT.COM

Saying yes when you want to say no can leave you feeling like you've been forced into doing something you didn't want to do. It doesn't feel good. For example, you may say yes to handing out flyers for an event supporting your church, but you don't agree with everything your church does anymore. So while it's a nice thing to do for your religion, you're now helping to promote an idea you don't necessarily believe in. Whether you've been pressured to go with the flow or you were raised to be agreeable, if you can't say no in your relationship, you're not going to be able to say yes to yourself.

You can practice saying no before you ever actually use the word. In fact, you can use it in your own life by figuring out some things you're not really into but you're tolerating anyway. Baczynski says, "Sometimes it's not even literally saying no, it's just dealing with things that irritate you—like a squeaky drawer. It's about valuing your own sense of comfort, well being, and joy."

There are also alternatives to saying no, like "Not now" or "I'm not okay with that." You can always say that you just can't do something at this point in your life (start with "I'm sorry" if you want to add a little extra sympathy). You don't owe an explanation after you say no, either. So be careful if you choose to give one anyway. An explanation opens the door for people to find ways to change your no. But no matter what you say, you need to be firm and consistent.

Once you learn to say no, you'll see no is one of the most liberating words you know. No?

What Makes a Relationship Toxic?

There are many types of bad relationships that don't have clear labels, but the actual definition of a toxic relationship is a relationship between two or more people that is unsafe and dysfunctional. This is different from a dysfunctional relationship, or any other relationship that isn't working, in that it is physically or emotionally unsafe to stay in it. A toxic relationship takes negative emotions to the extreme, but both toxic and dysfunctional relationships are characterized by negative behaviors that are constant or normalized in the relationship. These behaviors include (but are not limited to) acting jealous, insulting, demeaning, and yelling. They involve control, domination, narcissism, and insecurity that can be emotionally, and possibly physically, damaging. In these relationships, there is generally inequality in the expectations of the roles played by each person—for example, one person gives while the other takes.

Toxic relationships affect us on a myriad of levels. They can affect our psyche, making us continuously question what we're doing and who we are. They can make us question ourselves because our intuition is telling us one thing, and our brain is telling us another (Hint: always go with your gut). Our self-confidence can be affected when we're told we are crazy, wrong, or can't survive on our own. And because we're stressed out about the relationship, we can see tangible manifestations of the toxicity too. We may get physically ill with fever or depression. We may not want to get out of bed some days because the relationship affects our thinking, work, and personal life. And we can start to hate ourselves because we aren't being true to ourselves, especially if we think that we're compromising our values and beliefs.

WARNING AHEAD: TOXIC RELATIONSHIP

If you're wondering what a toxic relationship looks like, here are some examples.

- A business partner who devalues your input, claiming your ideas are "worthless."
- A friend who is extremely jealous of you and hurts your reputation by gossiping about you.
- A relationship that makes you feel bad most, or all, of the time.
- A family member who uses lying and manipulation to isolate you from your friends or other family.
- A friend or family member who harshly criticizes you. They may say things like, "You're so unmotivated, you'll never accomplish anything in life."
- A relationship with a family member where you are not allowed to be, or act, in a way that feels true to yourself.
- A friend who always has to be right and discounts everything you say as wrong.
- A relationship where all your energy goes toward said relationship, and you feel drained.

♀ 🔒 ♂

Real-Life Break Ups

"Staying in a toxic relationship required me to give up or put on the back burner many important parts of myself. It also meant I neglected other important relationships with friends, due to the jealousy and needs of that person. Not only were they controlling and overwhelmingly critical of me, the worst part of it was that I honestly began to doubt myself and think that it was largely my fault." —Erin

🔒

Unhealthy Relationship Types

A relationship doesn't have to be toxic for it to no longer be a good relationship. Any relationship that doesn't allow us to enjoy ourselves is likely in need of a makeover. Toxic or not, these unfulfilling relationships can be about many things, like a business that doesn't allow us to evolve with the times (or ourselves). It can involve a parent who punishes us for making adult decisions they don't agree with. It can happen when we disagree with the doctrine of our religious community. If you want to make a change and the relationship is holding you back, it's only going to get more frustrating if you stay.

Even if your unfulfilling relationship doesn't fit into one of those examples, if anybody makes you question your sanity, feel like you'd rather shut down than join in a conversation, or feel bad about yourself in any way, or if the person embarrasses you in front of others, hides things, or doesn't let you do you, "Danger, Will Robinson, danger."

It takes at least two people to be involved in a relationship, so even if you don't see yourself as the toxic part of the relationship, you still need to take ownership of your role. There's some dynamic between the two of you that causes a relationship meltdown. Bad relationships range in intensity and can show themselves in vary-ing degrees. In fact, as you read this, you probably will see elements of toxicity even in your non-toxic relationships. When these nega-tive interactions happen on occasion, it's not something to worry about. But when this is an ongoing, continuous way of connecting, it's time to cut the cord.

If you can identify your uncle, your close friend, your trainer at the gym, or anyone else in the relationships below—it's time to think about change.

THE NO-"WE"-IN-"ME" RELATIONSHIP

A relationship that is all about me (as in one person), not we (as in us), is the kind of relationship that generally involves a whole lot of narcis-sism and a not a lot of collaboration. The user (the person soaking up all of the relationship energy) has somehow made this entire relation-ship all about their needs, problems, and solutions.

It's easy to enable this type of one-sided relationship. Think about if you've ever been coerced or manipulated into doing things that don't make you happy. It could be going out to a bar the night before a big test, or hanging out with your best friend's boyfriend every time you want to see your best friend. It can happen when you were hired for a specific job but your boss has assigned you to do other tasks instead (and they weren't a part of the actual job description). It can even be that you don't want to look in the mirror and see yourself as a woman any longer, but your family refuses to acknowledge you when you iden-tify as a man.

These relationships can be very demanding. Your parent might encourage you to always be available, like a Denny's. They may also come with the expectation that you will drop everything for the "user" at once and with haste. You may not feel like you have the power to change things, but you do have the right to be in charge of your own life.

Antidote: *To let go of this type of relationship, you may need to make the break up about their needs and how you can't possibly ever meet them.*

I once had a friend who, if she called you her "good friend," expected you would drop everything to be there for her—no matter what. If I wasn't available when she needed me, then I felt like I was doing something wrong. Suffice to say, this relationship was mentally exhausting as well as anxiety producing.

I eventually ended the relationship. I told her I couldn't be what she needed me to be, and I didn't want to let her down any longer (again, making it about her). While this pissed her off—after all she had trusted me to be *that* friend—eventually we were able to become acquaintances again. Still, I had to let her go so she would stop relying on me to fill some other void in her life. I'm not sure she ever found what she was looking for, but I hope she learned that whatever it was wasn't about everyone else. I got back to reclaiming me, so that I could share myself with other we's.

THE ARGUMENTATIVE RELATIONSHIP

This relationship is all about the fight. But unlike Fight Club, what goes on between the people in this type of relationship never seems to stay between them. In the case of non-romantic relationships, there's no makeup sex to help you both feel better. Fights can be as small as disagreeing about what the best movie of all time is (of course it's *The Princess Bride*) or as big as arguing over the end-of-life care for your dad. In this relationship, there's only one thing you can completely agree on: you always disagree.

If somebody sends you into a tizzy every time you say how you're feeling, then it may be time to stop the insanity. You find these types of relationships between groups of friends where not everyone in the clique is clicking (think of the movie *Mean Girls*). In familial situations, it's likely more of a problem if it's happening all of the time, and not just when there's a major life event (like a funeral or wedding), when emotions tend to magnify. You may also see this with a bad choice in business partner. Or you may fight over cats and dogs (literally) every time you see your next-door neighbor.

Antidote: To let go of this type of relationship, you may need to make it absolutely clear that you are not going to continue to communicate through anger.

Whether it's because they live next door, they're in your bloodline, or you work with them, you can't always easily part ways with someone you disagree with all the time. Still, if there's a person in your life who makes you itch with irritation, then it's time clear that relationship up.

Try writing them an email asking to come up with a joint solution—one in which you both work together to change the way you interact. Or, perhaps you come up with a mutual list of "rules" that you both can abide by in order to get along. You may also agree that each time you get angry, you step away from one another. Then, after taking twenty-four hours to think things through, you reconvene and address the situation from a place of less anger and hurt.

THE BAH-HUMBUG RELATIONSHIP

Fueled by negativity, this relationship is a real downer. It may involve a person who has nothing positive to say, about you and everything else. In a working relationship, it may happen when your boss puts you in a position of power and then shoots down your decisions. In families you can see this too. For instance, you plan a family reunion and then your sister tells you how much better she could have planned it. In any relationship, it means that no matter what choice you make, it's never the right choice.

Being around someone who thinks you could always do or be better is maddening. They may embarrass you in front of other people or put you down whenever the two of you are alone. They may be critical of your every action and question your every intention. They may ask you to justify things that don't need justification. In their presence, you feel judged, stifled, and criticized. You don't need their review to be a better person, but they give it to you anyway. If they make you feel like you're doing everything wrong, then you need to learn to make right by you.

Antidote: *To let go of this type of relationship, try killing it with kindness. Even when they tell you that you couldn't possibly manage without them—stay positive and move along.*

You can find negative Nancies anywhere in your life. This may be a negative member of your community or even the barista that you visit every morning before work. It can be a best friend who doesn't want you to do anything for yourself or a parent who believes they know what you need better than you. If someone is bringing you down all the time, even in a joking manner, things need to change.

In these situations, find a mantra before you head into the break up. Talk with people who believe in you and can help you feel confident about making a change. To help counteract all the negativity, you can also write down a list of the positive things in your life.

THE GUILT-TRIP RELATIONSHIP

This relationship is typical between primary caregivers and their offspring. Guilt trip relationships aren't about miscommunication; instead they're about subtextual communication. That means the other person makes requests of you with the implication that by not fulfilling their requests, you are negatively impacting their life. They draw on close bonds to create a sense of obligation.

Antidote: *To let go of this type of relationship, you may need to be willing to let go of anyone who enables the*

*relationship. Since this relationship is about using guilt, or a
sense of obligation, to control your actions, complete disconnection is the way to reconnect with yourself.*

Therapy can be really helpful when going through this type of
break up. Not only can therapy help you talk through your situation, it
can provide you with the tools to move forward without feeling guilty
for your desire to disconnect from your "obligation."

THE TURN-IT-AROUND-ON-YOU RELATIONSHIP

This is a relationship with someone who can't actually hear you
because they are so caught up in being heard. When you explain to
them how they hurt you, they mince your words and make their own
thought salad out of the remains. Then, they throw them back at you
to make it seem like you're the one hurting them. They may overre-
act when you bring up your feelings or deflect what you're saying by
avoiding the situation altogether. Often in these relationships, you
find yourself apologizing or comforting your partner for how you
were feeling. You wind up taking care of everyone but yourself.

Antidote: *To let go of this type of relationship, you will need
to make sure you are heard. Have the other person repeat back
to you what you just said (and vice versa) so that you can make
sure words are not being lost in translation.*

You can see this type of relationship with parents, siblings, and
other people you have long-standing miscommunication practices
with. A business partner who won't own her part of the failed business
is another example of where this relationship plays out. In communities, when you're trying to do something that goes against the grain, like
state a different point of view from the community "mission" or express
unhappiness with one of its members, your community may feel that it's
you, and not their ideas or members, that needs to change.

THE KEEPS-YOU-GUESSING RELATIONSHIP

In this relationship, words and actions don't stick. You can't rely on the person because they've made themselves unreliable. And in being unpredictable, you feel insecure about where you stand in the relationship. You may question what you did wrong or what you could have done differently. This is another of those relationships that makes you doubt yourself, even if you have no doubt that what's going on is not right.

Antidote: *To let go of this type of relationship, you will need to be open to hearing the other side of the story. Even if you don't believe them, you need to let them feel heard. Perhaps something really did come up, or maybe you did do something to hurt them. If their reasons are legitimate, then you'll both need to find a way to communicate better. If their reasons feel like they are more about control and manipulation, then you will likely need a clean and total break. Be prepared to own your part, or at least to stop fighting them regarding their story, and try to break up with dignity and respect for one another.*

Say you made plans with your best friend to meet for lunch and she cancels at the last minute for no apparent reason. And this isn't the first time she's bailed on you in the eleventh hour. Or your mom tells you she's going to watch your kids every Saturday, but each time Saturday rolls around, she's nowhere to be found. Depending on your level of entanglement, you may be able to walk away. But if you have known them for many years or relied on them in the past, you need to say something to stop the cycle or end the relationship.

While this isn't necessarily a sign of dysfunction, it's definitely annoying. Unpredictable behavior typically doesn't start at the beginning of a relationship; in most instances, it happens after trust is built. Still, it can leave you obsessing over what happened to this person's "reliability factor." Unpredictable behavior doesn't only suck, but also sucks the life out of a relationship.

Figuring Out Your Unhappiness Level

Maybe your relationship doesn't fit one of these descriptions, or maybe it fits more than one. The point is, if the relationship you're in makes you feel like you're drinking poison Kool-Aid, there's a good chance you are in a toxic relationship. And all the pretending in the world can't make that change. So stop pretending and make a change.

The best way to change a relationship is to make changes in yourself first. Break up with the way you are, and make up the ways you want to be. When you start to recreate your own patterns, others will join in, or not. If they don't, then you can see where the problems continue to fester, and you can choose how to define the break up more clearly.

The bottom line is, if you can never say no to the other person because she or he pouts, whines, gets pissed, sends you a barrage of text messages until you change your mind, disappears on you, or bad-mouths you to other people, it's time to rethink your role in the relationship. And if you aren't on board with how the relationship is going, it's time to jump overboard.

If you don't think your relationship is fair, it probably isn't.

Why Ending a Bad Relationship Is a Good Idea

Bad relationships don't help you thrive (even if they have, in the past, helped you survive). But just because a relationship is unhealthy or uninspiring doesn't mean the relationship didn't serve some of your needs. All relationships have their benefits. Before you dive in to the break up, be specific about what you got out of the relationship. Make a list of the reasons you've stayed. For example, your boss abuses you in the same way your parents did, and this is oddly comforting. Maybe hanging out with your best friend's children makes you feel less guilty for never having the children your parents hoped you'd have. Perhaps your religious affiliation gives you something to do every Sunday morning, and you like to have a place to go. Once you figure out what you get out of the relationship, you can figure out how to replace that "special" something.

You may also find ways to have empathy for the toxic people in your life. That doesn't mean you give in to their insecurities, but toxicity usually comes from a sense of not feeling deserving of love. Or it comes from a place of not feeling like anyone else will be there for them. Being narcissistic, negative, critical, dominating, overbearing, and disappointed is definitely a part of the problem, but usually the toxic person has a bigger problem they need to work on.

Breaking up, or talking about the break up, can generally be a push to either resolve issues or live with the consequences. Reconciling a toxic relationship isn't completely hopeless; however, it is hard to get out of the cycle of bad without first breaking it off completely. If you want them back, odds are you have a better chance of doing so by getting rid of the gunk first. You will gain more of their respect and more of your own power by taking a break verses sticking around and feeding fuel to their fire. If you don't leave the relationship, then your toxic person will always remember they can call your bluff.

After the break up, give it a month, or three, before you even think about contacting them again. If you choose to reconvene, maybe approach the first meeting with a short list of what you need to move forward. A list of what you need to see happen in order to be able to stay in the relationship will help you focus on fixing things. If a trial separation or a clear list of needs don't work, and you still can't say goodbye, then you can always limit the amount of time you spend together.

Even spending limited time together may not be a perfect solution. No change or break up is super simple. But you'll have more clarity after the break up. Find support and surround yourself with positivity in order to let go of the negative force(s) holding you back in your life. You can expect a fight until the end, so be prepared to fight with love and kindness if you can.

Ultimately, only you—and the recipient of your break up—know why your relationship is ending. You don't have to tell everyone that it's toxic. But if you're feeling like a servant to the relationship, it's time to become the master of your world.

Be your own Toxic Avenger.

CONSIDERATIONS FOR THE BROKEN UP

1. It takes two (or more) people to have an unhealthy relationship, so although you play an important role in the unraveling, the other person knows they need to own their role too.
2. Try to really listen to what is not working so you can work on ways to enjoy your other relationships more.
3. Don't fight the break up. It may be the best way to change the relationship as it stands.
4. Ruminate on what it is that makes you act the way you act. Is your role comforting to you in some way?
5. Appreciate the opportunity to learn from the relationship and say thank you for the other person's bravery and respect.
6. You will be okay too.

FOUR

Breaking Up Verses Taking a Break (Do You Need One?)

❝ *Relationships are like glass. Sometimes it's better to leave it broken than hurt yourself trying to put it back together.* ❞

—UNKNOWN

Simply uttering the words "break up" can instill a lot of anxiety in a person. The routine of a relationship is comforting and familiar. It can feel better knowing you have this security blanket in your life than it might to get rid of a tattered rag. Plus, it's stressful, complicated, and mind-boggling to end a relationship that you had once taken comfort in or were excited by.

It's a lot to wrap your brain around, this idea that you are ending something that you may never have again or that you don't ever want to have again. But by the time you get to breaking up, or taking a break, you should have already aired your frustrations, provided a simple list of deal breakers, and assessed what you can live with and what you're willing to lose. You may have even given yourself a timeline for turnaround (with or without the other person's knowledge), but things might not seem to be getting any better. Or you may have decided that you're not done, but you need some time away in order to come back to a place of understanding and compassion with this person.

Sometimes we think a break will allow us to see things more clearly and make it easier to figure out the boundaries of the relationship, without going to the extremes of a break up. For those people who need it, a break can improve a broken relationship.

Is This a Break Up or Just a Break?

The clear difference between breaking up and taking a break is the timeframe. When you decide to break up, time is an infinite number. You're not planning on speaking again in two weeks or even two years. There is no expectation of "getting back together" sooner or later, even if you really, really hope that you can reconcile. You start to figure out a life without the other person. If you're leaving a business, you think about your next endeavor. If you're leaving a community, you may think about going solo for a while or finding a group of people you feel more aligned with. If you're breaking up with a best friend, you may delete pictures on social media and box up mementos from your time together. With a break up, you don't set up a period of time that you will remain apart. It's not even a possibility, because considering the possibility of time apart taints the break up. With a break up, you mourn the end of a relationship so that you can move on.

On the other hand, taking an intentional break involves setting a timeline for change. There is a spoken agreement that there is a chance, in the not-too-distant future, that this too shall pass. You don't necessarily make plans to move on in the same way you would after a break up. With a break, there is a set amount of initial time apart, and then a designated date to discuss the state of the relationship as it was and as it will be.

Breaks happen for all sorts of reasons. Perhaps you can't deal with the person or situation right now because too much is going on in your life. You want to be able to have a relationship with them, but you need to devote time to other things right now. When their neediness gets in the way of your needs, a break can be in order.

Sometimes initiating a break may be all you need to rejuvenate the relationship. It can be a reminder of how much you actually like a person and make you realize you forgot to appreciate them for a while. For example, you enjoy a particular gym class, but it's just getting boring because it's the same routine every week. So you take a break from that instructor, until the routine feels fresh again.

Or you take a break because you really don't want to break up, but you can't get out of a relationship rut. Perhaps you and your best friend have been arguing over her boyfriend for the past two years. Or maybe you and your mother know that you love each other a lot, but you need some space to get away from the same old song and dance. You take a break so you can distance yourself from the relationship long enough to return to it with a stronger sense of self.

Sometimes break ups become breaks, and breaks become break ups. Whether you opt for a break up or a break, you really can't predict how it's going to end or begin again—no matter how hard you try.

Not All Break Ups Are Forever

Even if you had every intention of staying broken up, break ups may become breaks due to forces beyond your control. Some relationships are brought back together through death, marriage, or other life changing events. I wanted to find a way to reconvene with my best friend after our break up about a boy. It was her cat's congestive heart failure that finally brought us back together.

I've broken up with a few friends, and two "best" friends, over the course of my decades. In almost all instances, we spoke again at some

THE THREE R'S OF A BREAK UP

Before you decide you're going to try to get back together, make sure you've revisited the Three *R*'s of a Break Up.

Reassess: Consider the relationship again. Is this something you want to revisit?

Reevaluate: Weigh the pros and cons of the relationship. What worked? What didn't? Is it worth trying to work out the kinks?

Realign: Can you come together to find a middle ground?

point. In fact, in the case of my two best friends, I'm super tight with one of them (and now the terms of our relationship are more clearly defined), and I am intermittently in touch with the other. In the second instance, we reconnected almost a decade after we broke up at our ten-year high school reunion. The former felt like a break, but the latter was definitely a break up.

Break or break up, I didn't go into either of them knowing the outcome. In fact, they both felt like break ups at the time. Still, the one that turned into a break went down like this:

Elle was my former roommate and closest girl friend. She ended our relationship over a misunderstanding about a boy who would become my future ex-boyfriend. Only after I made out with him all night long (which was a mess in and of itself) did I find out that she actually liked him. (At the time, she was in another place making out with another boy.) Still, it quickly escalated into a bad situation.

Before I knew what was happening, Elle had literally written me off. She sent me an email that ended our friendship and made me sound, and feel, like an awful human being. I couldn't talk to her, not because I didn't try, but because she wanted nothing to do with me. I withdrew into my own crazy world and lived life in a place of constant chaos for the better part of the next nine months.

When it ended, I didn't know how to handle never being friends again. We had a lot of mutual friends, so seeing each other was unavoidable. On top of that, we had a vacation booked in the midst of all of this turmoil. Because it involved another friend, and we are both stubborn, we decided to take the vacation anyway. The three of us talked enough to get through the planning of the trip, and, eventually the trip itself. It was quite possibly the most non-relaxing tropical island vacation, after which we stopped speaking again. Elle also stopped showing up at mutual friends events if she knew I would be there.

I hoped that Elle and I would find a time and a place to get back together. When I asked my friends what they thought I could do, they would tell me to give her space. So I gave her space. And then, one day, her five-year-old cat died unexpectedly of congestive heart failure. I wanted to call to offer my condolences, but our mutual friends advised me against it. I wanted to listen to them and respect her space, but I also wanted to check in on Elle. I texted her to ask if it was okay to call, and she said yes. She was, after all those months, actually really glad to hear from me. It took a few calls to start talking about what had happened to end our relationship. But once we did, we could move on in a better place and with a newfound respect for our friendship.

The break also gave us a chance to talk about our issues. Because we were both heavily invested in having a relationship again, we listened to one another with a deeper level of empathy. We talked about how she was cruel to me and about things she felt I did to her. We agreed to keep each other in check if these behaviors began to creep back into our relationship. The break provided us our own system of checks and balances. It still helps us today when we hit relationship obstacles. We can use our words and be honest with one another, and

DO YOU BREAK UP OR TAKE A BREAK?

"My break ups are always break ups. I'm a scorched earth, burned bridge kind of guy."

"I have never taken a break. It has always been clear when it was time to change the relationship into something else. Breaking up doesn't always mean an end to any part of the relationship. It evolves. That being said, some were clear good-byes. And just once—I saw someone wrestle with the idea of a relationship. And I created space for both of us, stretching time, gaining full freedom, and within that we came together."

"If you had to break up once, you might as well leave it broken."

"It depends on how much clarity you have about boundaries. I think the reason a lot of us need to take a break is to see what it's like to not have that person nearby, so we can then opt into the boundaries that feel right for the new relationship—if there is going to be a new relationship. I think the break is a step in setting the new set of boundaries."

we can call each other out when we need to. And because we know what it's like to not be around for each other, we consciously choose to stay connected.

Why Breaks Work

A break is a good option when you really don't want things to end but you need a chance to begin again. If you are certain this is a person you want in your life (at least in some capacity), a break most definitely works. If you're unsure, a break may be all you need to be certain.

Breaks don't work in every relationship, but they do work in some cases. And because you've hit bottom, you can take your time to see if there's a chance to make the relationship tops again.

However, if you're sure that it's a break up you're aiming for, then you're probably better off not thinking about ways to reconcile. But even if the break up eventually does turn into a break, both breaks and break ups are chances to reevaluate the ways and means of a relationship and to determine if and how your relationship will take shape in the future.

In fact, in an unscientific survey of my close friends, most of them agreed that when the break up was in a romantic relationship, it was over for good. But when the break up was in a non-romantic relationship, they sometimes found all they really needed was a break. Perhaps it's because there is no actual rubbing of penises and vaginas together, but there seems to be a lot more room for forgiveness when a relationship isn't sexual.

Breaks work because they are a chance to reassess the relationship. They give us time to reevaluate what we're getting out of the relationship versus what we need to get from the relationship. They allow us to realign our values so we can decide if we can indeed search for middle ground.

A break up that morphs into a break means that you have both decided it's better to find a way to make the relationship work than to be without the relationship. That means you're making the conscious decision to give this relationship a second chance. And because you both want this, you'll be more interested in investing time in the relationship. It means your heads and hearts are going to be in the right place.

A break may also help set up clear boundaries for the relationship moving forward. This can help make the relationship easier to navigate in the future. And if you decide to re-up a relationship and convert it from break up to break, you will gain clarity and insight into the relationship.

Think of it like spring break. Young adults use spring break as a chance to unwind and "go crazy" before they go back to school, work, or other responsibilities. Taking a "spring break" from your relationship can give you the time you need clean it up. The time apart can be a way to come back together and feel revitalized about the connection you share.

On a Positive Note

A positive note is a term used to describe an upbeat ending after delivering some pretty bad news. According to Illinois State University researchers Sandra Metts, William R. Cupach, and Richard A. Bejlovec, relationships have a better chance of reconciliation if they end on a positive note.[1] After a break up, an example of a positive note would be wishing them luck and telling them you will always hold a space for them in your heart. Or it maybe telling them you hope they find true happiness and inner peace.

In their research, "I love you too much to ever start liking you," Metts et al looked at a variety of ways people end romantic relationships. The team found that by ending a relationship on a positive note, you have a better chance of getting along again later on.

They studied a number of techniques people use (including withdrawal, ending things on a positive note, manipulation, and through direct communication) and found the kinder the person was during the break up, the better the break up went. And, if they were friends prior to the end of the romantic relationship, a positive tone had a direct impact on their future relationship, and meant they could likely be friends again.

The team also examined how the conversation went down. Was there a face-to-face interaction or an avoidance of one (known as distance cueing)? What they found was that both the technique used and the type of conversation held played a role in determining how ex-couples engaged later on.

The results? While relationship talk was the most difficult for the person doing the breaking up, it was also best for the person being broken up with. Sure, the person doing the disengaging face-to-face had to endure the feelings of anger and guilt that could arise from the receiver, which in turn could slow down the process, but it also indicated a higher level of respect for the party being broken up with. Distance cueing was seen as selfish, prioritizing only one person's needs to be free, and, in effect, devaluing the other person.

Ultimately, meeting face-to-face was not only seen as a positive tone strategy, but it also allowed for the best types of resolutions. Besides giving the recipient of the break up a chance to be heard, it showed genuine care.

What it comes down to: How you choose to end the relationship can determine the chances of its success in the future. So, if you're certainly uncertain about whether this is a break or a break up, talk about the end of the relationship face-to-face and end the converstaion on a positive note. This way, you have the most opportunity for success down the road.

Weighing the Pros and Cons

A break up is like a car crash. At first you're not quite sure what just happened. Before you can completely clear your head from the fog and the wreckage, you need to remove yourself from the situation. Only once you've recovered, can you get a chance to see what the damage was and if it's worth repair.

And while you wait to find out how much damage was done, you think of reasons for everything (whose fault it was, how it could have been avoided, how you could have been safer). There are going to be reasons to get back together, and there will likely be valid reasons to stay apart. A break up is a good time for self-evaluation. Even if you didn't initiate the break up, taking time to understand why it happened can put both the relationship and your way of relating into perspective. And it gives you a chance to look at the role you played in the ending of the relationship. You may not like how you acted, or reacted, and you may see some ugly in yourself that needs fixing.

When you're considering a return to any relationship, it's important to weigh the pros and cons of breaking up versus taking a break. Take a look:

PRO: You have new insight.

CON: But it may be too late to fix the past.

PRO: A break is a good chance to regain your individuality.

CON: Individuality is a great thing, but treading into territory where you don't need anybody or anything can be harmful to your personal growth and development. It's important to make sure you don't isolate yourself entirely while you're isolating yourself from the end of a relationship.

PRO: Taking a break from a relationship can help you grow together and can add to your personal growth.

CON: You may grow apart.

PRO: The relationship won't be the same as it was before. The relationship will hopefully change for the better, and you will feel more authentic.

CON: It can be unrealistic to grasp the concept that someone simply can't change. It's a tough realization to know that you cannot change the relationship.

PRO: If you can't live without each other and are willing to get back together, that means there are important reasons this relationship feels necessary.

CON: It could just be the other person misses what you did for them. And they may only be willing to make up to continue to use you for their needs. You both may be too codependent.

Now it's time for you to make your own list. What are the pros and cons for breaking up versus taking a break in your relationship?

In the Meantime

Whether or not you get back together, you will need to decide what to do in the interim. For example, do you remain in contact with your sister over certain things, like your mother's failing health, or do you only speak to her if your mother dies? If you and your ex–business partner still have bills to pay, do you both deal with it, or does one of you handle the details? If your best friend is being honored at your former church, do you still attend the ceremony, or do you celebrate her in a private ceremony at your own home?

And what do you do when it comes to social media when a relationship is pending? Do you plan to remove them from the Facebook facet of your life, or let them quietly idle in the unfollow section of your feed? And if you plan on taking out the big guns by blocking them from your world, do you let them know what you're about to do?

Whatever you decide, these are things you may want to think about before you break up, especially if you're looking at the status of your relationship as "pending" or "complicated." As Michael, a Facebook friend, told me, "I put my sister on my restricted list temporarily without telling her why." (She had posted something insensitive.) "She got very upset at the demotion and completely unfriended me, which makes me sad. So, always tell."

And what do you do if you run into each other? Do you completely ignore one another as if you never had a relationship? Or do you smile and nod and move on your way?

Sometimes relationships are brought back together through breaks, and sometimes they are not. Either way, this is an important opportunity for improvement and growth. This is a chance to work on yourself, in and out of the relationship and a chance to work on your other relationships too. And it's an occasion to decide what's truly important to you and for you.

CONSIDERATIONS FOR THE BROKEN UP

Want to see this as a break rather than a break up?

1. Back off: Don't text, call, or private message someone after they've broken up with you. Let them be.
2. Enjoy the time apart: Use this time to put things into perspective. It will allow you to see your part in the relationship as well as to really assess if this is a relationship you want to revisit.
3. No begging: If anything, begging induces pity. You're not looking for a pity party. You're looking for a way to be a part of this person's life.
4. Focus on you: Just like the other person has taken some time to focus on their needs, now that you have the freedom to see through the relationship, focus on what you need in your life.
5. Think about change: Before the break up, there were probably more hints or flat-out signs that this relationship was going south. What do you need to change to be in this relationship? Are you willing to make those changes?
6. Don't be a doormat: You don't need to be in a relationship with someone who sets restrictions on how you need to act or who you need to be in order to be around them. While changing bad habits is important, not being able to be yourself isn't going to work for you either.

FIVE

Best Friends Forever No More

"Friendship is like a glass ornament, once it is broken, it can rarely be put back together in exactly the same way."

—CHARLES KINGSLEY

You don't go into a friendship thinking it's going to end, and definitely not that it's going to end terribly. Most of the time, friendships start out as the best of both worlds. It provides a chance to be intimate, silly, honest, sweet, angry, ugly, and deep with another human being without all the sexual trickiness that gets in the way. Friendship is an opportunity to practice love without being in love. It's also a chance to learn life lessons about growing, up and apart. Often friendships change, or disappear without a peep. Other times they end abruptly, or intentionally.

We don't think a lot about what happened to those friendships that ended naturally, over time. We accept that we've changed, grown up, had families, or moved to different cities. We focus on our new lives and careers, and because our interests no longer align, we make new friends who we can relate to better. It's easier to accept the end of friendships that fizzle, or fade away.

It can be difficult to understand that we have a choice when it comes to friendship. But we do. We can be in it, or we can get out. We have the right to choose to end a friendship, and making that choice can be empowering. It's not only romantic partners who get so absorbed in the routine of the relationship that the relationship itself starts to feel stuck. There is always a way out. Especially if we can feel taken advantage of, undervalued, or bored in the relationship. Making a clear choice to end a friendship can signal a change in perception in your own life. It can show you that you've got this, that you're in control.

It doesn't matter who did what to whom; when you have to end a friendship, it usually sucks. And the longer the friendship, the more likely the break up will be an extraordinary show—of courage or cattiness. But life is too short to let a friendship bring you down.

Good Friend/ Bad Friend

Like brushing your teeth, exercising, and eating your veggies, good friendships are important for a healthy, long life. Good friends are dependable, honest, there for you in a pinch, and respectable listeners, and they won't gossip about you behind your back. Research proves that we need these types of people in our lives. Overall, people with strong social networks have been found to live longer lives—especially after traumatic events including cancer or heart attacks.[1] Strong social support can also help to lower blood pressure, promote brain health, delay the physical impairments of aging, and enhance our ability to deal with stress.[2]

It may come as no surprise that bad friendships do the opposite, wearing you down, tearing you up, and even making you eat more.[3]

Negative social interactions can also impact our health in other ways. A 2011 study done by UCLA's School of Medicine found that negative interactions increased the levels of inflammation-causing proteins that have been linked to cancer, depression, heart disease, and high blood pressure.[4]

That doesn't mean a fight (or two or three) with a friend will kill you, or that you should immediately halt all communication. But it does mean you should be wary of excess arguments.

Then there's also the emotional damage of a negative friendship. These types of relationships can lower our self-esteem and make us feel pretty worthless. They can cause us to feel extreme emotions, like enraged or depressed, and a bad friendship can make us doubt our ability to choose good people to surround ourselves with in life.

It gets even more confusing if the friendship that once helped us flourish now makes us recoil. We may not be able to see where the turning point happened. Or even if we do, we don't always understand how someone we were once so close to can feel so distant.

Even though we know these relationships need to end, ending a relationship with someone who was once a good friend can be stressful in the short-term and the long run. Of course, the length of time you've been in each other's lives may play a role in the lengths you're willing to go to salvage the friendship. As we get older, having friends who have known us forever and seen us through good times and bad is valuable and rare. And because we place a lot of value on our friendships, needing to end one can make us feel even worse than a romantic break up. We may think things like if we couldn't keep a friendship afloat, how could we possibly make other relationships last? These negative thoughts are not only damaging but also can destroy us from the inside out.

What we can learn through the heartache and pain is the value of friendship. Sometimes we find that it's high enough that we can't actually place a value on it. And when we realize that a friendship devalues us, it's time to make a change.

Real-Life Break Ups

"Sia was my best friend all through high school. We were often asked if we were sisters, and we most definitely tortured her brother as if we were siblings. I loved her like family, maybe more, and spent most of my free time with her. But when we went away to college, things changed.

After a phone argument that had to do with her ex-boyfriend and me watching *The Simpsons*, we stopped talking. We didn't officially break up, although I remember she said something along the lines of not doing this (friendship) anymore. It seemed easy for her to just choose to let me go, and maybe at the time I deserved it (I had been mean to more than one friend in high school).

I looked at it as a big fight that we chose not to resolve. She went on to become even closer with the other girls we grew up with, and I went my separate way. We're still cordial, on the verge of becoming even friendlier, but the 'unofficial' break up changed our relationship. I can count on two hands the number of times I've spoken to Sia since our friendship ended twenty-two years ago. And there are days, still, that I wish it hadn't happened at all. But managing to at least stay in each other's lives, albeit peripherally (we occasionally text and say we should talk), has been an acceptable consolation prize for the end of a long-standing friendship.

Still, the break up was devastating, especially when I saw her a few years later at a college event and she introduced me to her new best friend by saying, 'This is Jamye, my best friend from high school. And this is Sheri, my best friend in college. Wow, past and present best friends in one place.' I felt like an object and not a person, and I remember being sick to my stomach.

Because I had placed such a high value on our friendship, that statement took me to a new low. It was as if I was punched in the face by the fact that Sia had moved on. She didn't have the same space for me in her life, and what I valued in our relationship (our secret language, our conversations, our desire to protect one another) was something that wasn't there any longer. While it hurt to end the friendship, I knew we had made the right decision.

It's not always that cut and dry, but ending a friendship doesn't mean we have to forget what it was like to have that person as a friend. In fact, I still enjoy what Sia and I once had, and I wouldn't change a thing about our relationship all throughout high school. Her friendship was an integral part of my life, and it inspired me to want to meet other people and enjoy other relationships similar to the one I had with her." —Jamye

● ● ●

"When I first moved to the city where I live, I became friends with a girl during orientation for school. It turned out that she was originally from my hometown and went to my rival high school. I didn't know her growing up, but we had friends in common. I remember thinking when I met her, 'We're either going to be best friends, or she's crazy, or both.' Well, the final option (both) turned out to be true for a while, until it became clear that 'crazy' was too much for me to handle. I tried to slowly extricate myself from the friendship, but that didn't work. And all my friends just kept telling me to walk away, but I felt so guilty (and I was a little concerned that I might cause boil-your-bunny *Fatal Attraction* craziness if I actually 'broke up' with her). Ultimately, about one and a half years after I met her, I did finally 'break up' with her. I used yet another bad life decision she was making as my excuse, telling her that I could not stand by her while she was making this decision, and I was sorry I wasn't a better friend." —Katie

🔒

Why Breaking Up with a Lover Is Easier Than Breaking Up with a Friend

Ending a friendship can hurt more than ending a romantic relationship. Whether she's been your best friend since first grade or the girl you met last year at that Halloween party, friendships can be life-changing events. But just because you once had matching jewelry declaring your friendship forever doesn't mean it will always be that way.

There's a lot of support around, and songs about, breaking up with a lover. If you Google break ups, the results all seem to talk about affairs of the heart. Many of us have heard the phrase "Boyfriends/girlfriends come and go, but good friends are forever." While that sounds solid, it can also be some anxiety-producing bullshit.

It's easier to find closure in a romance that we tried and tried to make work than a friendship we thought we could fix by ignoring certain parts or hoping they would go away.

In fact, while it may help us to feel empowered to break up in romantic relationships, ending a friendship doesn't necessarily fuel that same empowerment. Sentiments like "friendships are forever" can make us feel guilty about not wanting to be friends with someone anymore, especially when we continue to hear, see, or read that friendships last a lifetime.

Friendships can drag on a lot longer than other types of relationships. That's because a lot of these relationships are important for our personal growth and also because friends can be so interconnected that letting go of one person can change the entire dynamic of a network. When ending one relationship impacts an entire community, it can be really hard to rock the boat.

Ending a friendship is challenging when you share a social network, but it can also be challenging when you don't. If you have a long history of being in each other's lives or you've spent a lot of the most recent part of your life together, you are going to have a tough time choosing how to disconnect. It's not easy to end things with someone who once was your constant companion. However, constant companions aren't always constant. People die, move on, and make change all the time.

Why Friendships End

Many times issues in the friendship will be readily apparent. Your friend overstays his welcome on your couch and doesn't understand why he should pay a part of the rent. Or your girlfriend is endangering her health, or the welfare of other friends, by taking drugs, partying, and making bad decisions.

If it isn't blatantly obvious but you are always bitter when you think about this person, then make a list of the things you like about them and the things you don't. Then weigh the pros and cons (this works in any relationship). Ask yourself a couple of these questions: How long has it been since you've stopped getting along with your friend? Do you feel like you carry all the weight in the relationship? What about your friend's habits can't you stand? Does the beginning of her conversation continuously interrupt the middle of yours? Is she gossipy? Negative? Once you get a better understanding of what it is you feel is happening, you can put things into perspective and determine if there is any possibility to save the relationship.

Friendships can become endships when the relationship is a total drain on our emotional, mental, and/or physical well being. Whether it's because we are constantly fact-checking a friend who has turned to lying to get by or because we found out our friend has been saying some really mean things behind our backs, it's never easy to end what once was a good friendship (yes, it's way easier to end one that never really took off).

A friendship can turn into an endship over one person's inability to deal with being a "mutual" friend. It may be a case of self-absorption, as in a narcissistic relationship that has gone too far or a manic relationship that has blasted off to the scary side of crazy town.

You'll have to look at you too. How do you act toward and around this friend? Does your friend bring out your Jekyll or Hyde? Are you hot tempered, cold as ice, or indifferent to their annoyances? What buttons does she know how to push that bring you up to boil? Once you get into the details of the how you interact, you can see more of the minutia of what is and isn't working.

Real-Life Break Ups

"I enjoyed—well, some of the time—a friendship with a person who was incredibly charismatic and fun. They had so much energy. But when I really looked at the situation, I realized there was also a level of chaos with this person that I had to look at. And I couldn't take the chaos. So, I broke it off. What it fundamentally boiled down to was that I valued this one set of things that I was getting from the relationship, but then, the things it came with—the price was too high." —Marcia

● ● ●

"I broke up with a friend who actually felt more like a sister to me. When we met, I was drawn to her. She felt like she was already a part of me and I needed to know her.

What led to our initial break up was her husband cheated on her with somebody that he and I were friends with. I had no idea. Looking back, that was naive of me. But I truly never thought he'd do that. She felt betrayed by me for being friends with this woman and was upset when I wouldn't end my friendship with her. There was so much clouding any conversation we had about it that the conversations turned our love and respect into anger, resentment, and blame.

The friend break up was long and drawn out and confusing and weird. In the end, I think she threw in the final towel. But there was so much that led up to it. There were so many curveballs. So much trying again. Then distance. She ended up moving with her husband down to L.A., and after a few sad things happened in her life, I reached out again. We had a face-to-face in L.A. where I told her how sorry I was that everything went down as it did. I told her that I'd love to have her in my life but had no interest in having her husband in my life again.

However, she had made peace with him and they were moving on together. I didn't totally understand why and how but did understand that that decision would impact any chance we had of being friends down the line. For a long time, there was still the longing to find resolution on both our parts. We would share a few texts here and there, go on an outing to a museum. We tried catching each other up on our lives, but when I didn't invite her to my wedding reception because I didn't want him there . . . I never heard from her again." —Coyote

🔒

How to End a Friendship

You're not in high school anymore. Either you resolve your differences, or you don't. And if you don't, then you have several options when it comes to ending a friendship.

You can just let it slide from its former place of high friendship status to a place of lesser importance, especially if you're not big into confrontation. You can also become more involved in things that your friend doesn't like, for instance if she hates the bar scene and you spend your weekends at bars, you'll probably start seeing a lot less of each other. You can return phone calls less often and ignore texts for a while. Or you can outright tell your friend that you're not into her anymore and let the words sink in.

Friendships minus the "fri" happen all the time. It's a part of life and growth. When it comes to a friendship we once valued, how we end the relationship is as important as what we do to begin again.

OPTION ONE: MEET FACE-TO-FACE

Remember the positive-note research done by Metts, Cupach, and Bejlovec (discussed in Chapter Four) reminds us that ending a relationship face-to-face, and with compassion, provides the best outcome for closure or reconciliation.

Yeah, it may be daunting, and it's definitely difficult, but this option will provide you with the most definitive closure you can ask for. That's because both of you will be able to see and feel the impact of your words. Plus, it's the most open and honest way to show them that you care, even if your level of caring has diminished so greatly that you're ready to care a whole lot less.

In meeting face-to-face, wait until there are no big waves—like a funeral, a wedding, a new job, a friend's big party, a midterm or final, or a serious illness. If you do it during a really emotional time, then a break up conversation can become a whole lot of arguing without resolution. Don't break up a week after your friend's father dies or the night they found out that they flunked out of college for partying too hard. Try not to end the friendship at a party where you're celebrating another mutual friend's big promotion or birthday. In fact, don't end the friendship at a party ever, and never anytime that you're drunk or high. End the friendship when it's just the two of you and you're in a quiet and sober place.

Of course, if you have to get it out now, then do what you have to. But you may want to acknowledge the sense of urgency before you end it all. Tell them that while you know this isn't the best time to end your friendship, you aren't sure when the right time would be. Mention how it's been on your mind and you really need to talk about it. Own up to why it has to be now, and be honest about your own needs in the moment.

Don't get into the finger pointing of who did what and why. Instead refrain from being a big baby and be the bigger person. Even if you think there's a lot of blame, try to see both sides. There's no need to apologize for needing to end the relationship, unless you did something really shitty. Just make sure that both you and your friend understand these A, B, C's:

A. It's over.
B. These are the reasons why (be as concise as you can be here).
C. This is how you're going to handle it with your other friends.

Don't make plans for future dates, and don't be surprised if mutual friends get a little weird too. It happens. Just make sure you have clear boundaries and that the two of you understand the deal in ending the friendship.

A lot of times, it doesn't take hours of conversation to end a friendship, even one that took years to build. But it can take brutal honesty and a lot of willpower to not cave in to requests to make it better or to avoid saying sorry when you're really not sorry about it being over.

OPTION TWO: VIDEO CHAT OR PHONE

Sometimes you live across the country from the person you need to get away from, and just because you could wait until your paths cross again doesn't mean you want to. In instances where distance is a factor, phoning it in is a good idea. Sure, it's not as brave and personal as face-to-face, but when you physically can't do it or don't want to emotionally, a video chat or phone call are still better options than most of the others out there.

Talking via a real-time video chat allows you to see the person, but from the safe distance of not-in-the-same-room or state. It still allows you to read emotions and see expressions, only there's no awkward in-person meeting and greeting. Instead it's awkwardly done over the computer. And when you turn off the computer, you don't have to get in the car and drive home; you're already there.

If video chat doesn't work because you don't actually want to see your friend when you dump them, or because you don't have a personal computer to chat on, you can do it by phone. It still gives you a chance to speak to each other prior to ending things, and it allows you to listen to what the recipient has to say. Still, it's not as easy to read a person, even if they are super open, and it may not give you the complete feeling of closure. But it may.

OPTION THREE: WRITE IT DOWN

A note is a good way to communicate a lot of things you may find difficult to say otherwise. Especially if you're highly emotional about something a friend did and you need to find a way to create some added distance. Writing things down gives you a chance to think about what you want to say and precisely how you want to say it. Getting it out in words gives you a chance to explore your emotions without getting too emotional in a face-to-face conversation. By having the words written out in front of you, you can get all of your points across and make a very clear case about your decision.

Letters are forgiving. Because you have a chance to think through the words you choose, you can say really hard things more easily and with compassion. If you don't like somebody anymore, you can use words that convey your meaning in more flowery prose (or you can be direct, if that's your style).

With a letter, there is less back and forth arguing, and you can be sure that you've really thought out what it is you wanted to say. Of course, you have to decide if you will invite a response from the friend, or if you're just going to have a one-sided break up. You can also decide if you want to use the letter as a heads-up, so that when you do meet in person, you have a jumping off point. And if they write you back after all is said and done, you can read it, rip it up, or stick it in a drawer to open at a later date.

Or, you can write a letter for yourself (and never send it). It can help give you an idea of the points you want to hit when you do go in for the face-to-face talk. Or it can remind you, later on, how you felt before the friendship ended. However you use your words, writing them down can give you a lot of clarity.

OPTION FOUR: DO THE GRADUAL SAYONARA

This is an option when friendships are close enough that not making a point of shifting the relationship could be awkward, but you aren't so invested in one another's lives that you speak to each other all the time. If you are in a clique (like a sorority) and this person is part of your close group of friends, or if you know you will continue to see this person in your social circle, this is a gentler way to stop faking a friendship with them.

Slowly backing away usually works if both parties are not that interested in being friends but are interested in maintaining friendships with other people in the group. In order to back away slowly, you can start by limiting the amount of time you talk to each other when you do see one another. When you do talk, share less. Try not to share any intimate details about your life, especially anything that makes you feel vulnerable. Also, while you're saying less about your life, stop offering advice or suggestions on theirs. Don't make future plans, or even pretend that you hope to get together sometime soon. And decline any invitations to get together for a drink or to go to a concert.

As you grow further apart, you don't have to feel obliged to pick up the phone when they call, and you probably shouldn't text back right away either. While I'm not for playing games (outside of board games like Monopoly, Stratego, and Trivial Pursuit), it's important that they understand they are not a priority in your life. It may be hard at first, and you may feel like a bad person for blocking them out slowly, but sometimes one or both of you aren't truly ready to say goodbye. When slowly backing away, you may realize you don't need to break up completely to find a place for your friend in your life. Perhaps the gradual sayonara allows you to find a space in acquaintance-ville for you old-time friend.

OPTION FIVE: DISAPPEAR

Okay, I said it in chapter two—a disappearing act isn't cool. But I can't ignore it as an option. And while it won't work with a good friend, it does work with a casual acquaintance. But if they are just a casual acquaintance, you probably don't need to worry about the whole break up anyway. And sure, disappearing is definitely easy, but if you do it to a friend, you're a jerk.

I do mean to sound harsh. Sure, we've all disappeared from someone's life. But if this is someone you care (or cared) about, then you really need to think about why you can do this to them. Of course, if the friend is so abusive you don't know what else to do, then disappear. Stop answering their calls, texts, and emails. You may need to move away somewhere so they never find you. But if you can, or have to, disappear from a friendship, then you have bigger problems with, or than, this friend.

In the end, whatever path you choose, don't expect that your soon-to-be ex-friend is on the same page. He or she may or may not be down with your decision—not just your decision to break up, but also the way you go about handling it. Just remember: Meeting in person, or on video chat, provides the highest chance of satisfaction for both parties. Writing a letter provides one-sided satisfaction, while the gradual disappearance of said friendship or the quick non-goodbye is the easy way out.

While in-person is the best way to break up, I can't convince you to always do it that way. If I said I always broke up with people face-to-face, then I'd be a liar because it's not always an option, it's not always easy, and it's not always true. But that doesn't mean it's not the best option when it comes to showing respect in a relationship.

Real-Life Break Ups

"I had a friend write me a 'break up' letter and I was shocked. I remember at the time feeling, 'I feel like I just got dumped.' I was furious that there was no communication before the break, and the whole thing was based on a misunderstanding. I actually went through a mourning period." —Alex

Dealing with Your Other Friends

Oftentimes our friends are also friends with more of our friends, which makes breaking up with a friend a particularly tricky equation:

Friends + Friends − Friend = Awkward Friend Moments

You're almost certainly guaranteed to run into a friend, or twelve, who are still friends with your ex-friend. And because you are going to be around other people that may still like the person you're no longer friends with, you need to set up some really clear and firm boundaries around your break up. On top of that, you need to know how you will handle any violation. For example, if you tell your ex-friend you don't want to have any contact—email or otherwise—and they contact you, you may ignore it once, but if it continues, you have to decide if you will take action against them.

Tell your other friends about your agreement, too. If it's okay to be at a party with your ex-friend, let them know. (i.e. "We said we'd acknowledge each other with a nod, but not talk"). And if you get to said party and you can't keep your promise, it's your responsibility to not make a scene and just leave. Just like it would be their responsibility to do the same if they should feel the urge coming on. If you don't want to be invited to a party because your ex-bestie is going to be there, then don't make your other friends have to choose. It's pretty unfair to break up with someone and then expect your friends to do the same. And it's really not okay to expect your friends to get involved or to isolate your ex-friend from the group.

However, it is okay to tell your friends that you're not comfortable being in the same room/at the same party with your frenemy. And if you can't stand to be around them, don't. If you might both get an invitation, inquire about the guest list. And if they say that your yesterfriend is going to be there, then don't go. Don't make it a big deal or so uncomfortable that you force a choice on your other friends. Your break up is not their problem.

That might mean getting out of the way of your friends for a while. Let them have their relationships, and see them how and when you can. For instance, if a large group of friends is still friends with this one ex, make individual plans for a while. Or have a party at your place, and invite over a select group of peeps.

If you do run into your ex-friend, it's okay if it's awkward. But this doesn't mean you need to run the other way. Hopefully the two of you have made your peace and said your good-byes. As long as there has been closure, a pleasant smile and a nod should be all you need to keep on going.

If the break up wasn't clean or two-sided, then seeing each other will likely be difficult. If unresolved issues arise, the recipient may act passive-aggressively or outwardly cruel toward you. She may tell your other friends her side of the story, trying to make you look bad.

It could be best to avoid the recipient for a while. Once you've broken up, it's okay to disappear from their life, and it may even make the hurt heal faster. I had a friend break up with me and then disappear, and while it still hurt a lot, not seeing him was way easier than if I had run into him all the time. In fact, I don't know how I would have gotten over it if he were still hanging around.

Arnie felt like an instant best friend and most fun buddy (and truth be told, although we were never intimate, he was someone I could have seen myself dating), but he dumped me after he got a girlfriend.

Perhaps he would have done it in person if we were in the same state, but because I was in San Francisco and he was in New York, he did it by phone. I got the call while walking on Van Ness Avenue, right across the street from City Hall. He told me how he met a girl, and he really liked her. I remember being happy for him and a little bit sad for me, knowing that when I returned to New York, things would be different. I didn't have any idea how different they'd be, but I definitely wasn't ready for the whopper that came next. Arnie told me that because he had met this woman, we couldn't be friends anymore. No further explanation. No discussion. No apologies. Just, "I'm sorry, Jamye. I can't do this now."

I haven't seen, or spoken to, Arnie since that day. I don't know what I would do if I ever ran into him again, which honestly is highly unlikely since we don't live in the same state or even the same part of the country. I did write him an email expressing my hurt, but he held his boundaries, and when he responded, it was curt and consistent with his message that our friendship was over.

Looking back, while his approach wasn't the gentlest, it was direct. At the time, I felt like I could prove him wrong (about the not being able to be just friends part), but he was more insightful and honest than I was. He saw the things I wanted to deny. And by holding his ground and stepping out of my life, he gave me a chance to fill the void that he knew would be created by his being in this new relationship. And although I'm still sad that I lost the most fun friendship I'd ever known, I was glad he didn't dangle the pain in my face.

And as time has gone by, the friendship matters less, although as I type this, there's still a pain in my heart from where Arnie moved on. But I don't think about him most of the time.

I believe it's because Arnie was able to do the clean break. He never had me holding out hope for a change of heart. And he was concise and clear in his break up message, even when I really wanted him back in my life.

Odds are, almost anywhere you go, someone can share a story about a friend they don't talk to anymore. And by sharing these stories, it helps to see that no matter how different our paths are, we all share the common experience of making and ending friendships.

CONSIDERATIONS FOR THE BROKEN UP

1. You are not alone. Almost everybody has experienced at least one break up with a friend, and even those who have broken up with someone get broken up with too.
2. Take your time to process with your friends, your family, and others you can talk to about what they saw about the relationship and the roles you two played in the dissolution of your friendship.
3. Meditate or find other peaceful ways for introspection.
4. Try new experiences. Not only will this make you less likely to run into your frenemy, but you'll be also opening yourself up to making new friends too.
5. Write a letter to the person who broke up with you explaining your feelings. Even if you never send it, it can feel good to get it out.
6. You may be hurt, angry, disgusted, annoyed, relieved, or in shock, or perhaps you've just accepted the break up, but even with acceptance, you may not be okay with how it all ended. And that's okay.

SIX

Breaking Up with Family

« My family is my strength and my weakness. »
—Aishwarya Rai Bachchan

Family was originally defined as the descendants of a common ancestor, but that definition feels a bit limiting. Family is the people we are willing to drop everything for and go anywhere to be with. They are the collective whose honor we defend—sometimes until death—and whose love keeps us alive. We are brought up believing (if we are lucky) that family is our lifeline, our safe refuge, our history, and part of our identity. No matter if your family was waiting for you when you made your vaginal or cesarean debut or they welcomed you into their home sometime thereafter—family ties are supposed to be unbreakable.

Certain cultures (like Hispanic and Asian cultures) place family in the category of "be all, end all." Life without family is unfathomable and unquestionably not okay. This makes it even more difficult to imagine a split with someone in that core unit.

A familial break up can be devastating, heartbreaking, terrifying, and isolating. Ending a relationship with a family member can make you feel like Dorothy after the tornado, uncertain of how to find your way back home.

When you decide to cut ties with a person in your family, it can make you question your entire history. If you're breaking up with someone who helped you navigate life before you understood how to do things for yourself, you may feel like you're doing something wrong by not finding a way to make it right.

On the flip side, breaking a bad relationship pattern with a family member can be a relief. Finally some huge weight is being lifted off your shoulders. You no longer have to feel like you are sinking to the bottom of the ocean with no way up. You can breathe again. This can feel liberating, empowering, and scary.

Some family members never get with the program. It's worse when the people we feel are doing us wrong are our primary caregivers. If we are luckier, they are distant relatives whose lot in our lives isn't going to impact much more than a family reunion. This luck of the draw (meaning the family you were raised in) can result in emotionally, physically, or sexually abusive relatives as well as unaccepting family members who will go so far as to push God's will on their gay, lesbian, queer, trans, or questioning children, cousins, or siblings.

Familial relationships end for all sorts of reasons, including miscommunication, the desire for independence, divorce, the creation of new families, and enmeshment.

If we get into a difficult family situation, we can try to find a way to work within it or find some other group we can call family. And sometimes, in building our own safe familial unit, we have to dump some of the heavy load. Although we can't choose our blood family, we eventually get to choose if, and how, we want to deal with them.

The Intricacies of Familial Splits

Today, we live in a world of full of connections. We not only stay connected

WHAT DOES FAMILY MEAN TO YOU?

"The ones you go to the mat for. The ones you pick up their call whatever else is going on. The ones you bail out without complaint, or call AAA and use up your tow allowance for. They are the ones you escort home from danger, hold hands with in the hospital, return their emails, buy gifts for without a seasonal motive, update in your contact list, and don't lose touch with. The position is somewhat hereditary, but can be earned."

"Family is a unit of people that are genuinely there for one another."

"My related family has taught me that 'family' is love without condition or judgment. No matter how many crazy or dumb things I have done they've always been there and made me feel loved and supported. I hope to always do that for my husband, daughter, and family of friends and students."

"Not always blood . . . family are the people who cry for/with you, celebrate with you, understand you, and love you despite your neuroses. The ones who are still standing after any storm has passed."

"Those I love most; all of them friends. There is no one in my dwindling blood family I would want to know if I didn't have to."

in person via air, train, car, and bus travel, but our families can also be a part of our lives through social media, video chat, text, and phone.

In my opinion, connection is something we have too much of, which makes it harder to completely disconnect when things aren't going well. If we shut off our phones, log off of our profile pages, and stop checking emails, our closest friends and immediate family will usually notice and check in to make sure that we are all right. And when it feels like the only way to escape our family is to be chosen as part of Mars One, the idea of disconnection from a family member can seem impossible. But just because you were born into a family doesn't mean you're stuck with them for life. Sure, you can't remove them from your family history, but you can alter the present story.

This familial shift can be a tricky thing to navigate. Especially because we're told families, and definitely parental figures, do the annoying things they do because they love us and not because they want to hurt us. So what we may see as something done to hurt our sense of self, they may see as something said or done to protect us. For example, telling us that they don't like our boyfriend or girlfriend may be their way of saying, "We think you can do better because you are better." However, we may hear, "Once again, you screwed up a big, important choice in your life."

We don't always see things clearly, definitely not during our teen-age years when we often see their actions as cruel and unusual. While they may not see themselves as intentionally malicious, we don't care what they think. But, if we can stop the negative thoughts, with time and communication, we can figure out our family member's intention. And once we are clearer, we will have a better grasp on what we actu-ally need to do to make the relationship work, or not work, any longer.

Even bad relationships work on some level; if they didn't, we wouldn't be so invested in feeling bad about them. They work on feed-ing our insecurities, or perhaps our deeply held beliefs around how we think other people see us. They work to keep us down, because sometimes it's easier to be kept down instead of being held up to our own higher standards. If we rely on what others think of us, we don't necessarily have to expect too much of ourselves. It's not a great frame of mind to be in, but sometimes it feels safer to go with what you know than what you might learn about yourself if you jump out of that comfort zone.

♀ 🔒 ♂

Real-Life Break Ups

"My mom left my dad when I was a baby, so I didn't actually know my father. And it was really my grandmother who raised me. She walked me down the aisle for my wedding and passed away two weeks later.

I cut off my mom after my grandmother died. The last time I saw and talked to her was at my grandmother's memorial service. Our relationship started getting strained when I was around twelve or thirteen, and quite frankly it went downhill from there, getting worse as I got older. My mom began telling bigger and bigger lies to get what she wanted, and what I finally realized is that she's very narcissistic. She tries to break up the relationships of people she wants attention from. When I became a teenager and started hanging out more with my friends than my family, that's when all hell broke loose for me. I moved out when I was seventeen to get away from it, and a few weeks later my mom was diagnosed as bipolar, but she only took meds for two weeks before she went back to her same, crazy self. My mom is not good at taking care of her health in general.

It wasn't until I was twenty-one and watched my mom pick a fight with my aunt that I realized it was intentional. That was a turning point for me. I realized that all of these crazy stories that my mom was coming up with, these were intentional ways for her to destroy my grandmother's relationships with the rest of her family, so that my mom would look good in her eyes. It was hard to see my mom actively trying to destroy a relationship between my grandmother and her other child. My mom did a lot of damage between her siblings and her mom.

Once I realized I was over what she was doing, I pretty much stopped acknowledging her presence unless I had to. As cold as that sounds, I would mentally cut her out of the picture as much as possible. It was pretty simple, and ending the relationship was just a formality after my grandma died. I didn't need to say anything. I don't even really remember much about the details about that last trip. I don't remember saying anything specific, I just remember my husband and me leaving. And that was it. It had already ended so long ago in my brain, so my grandmother's memorial wasn't my ending point, is was just the official 'I don't have to have you in my life anymore.'

What I learned is that no matter what the relationship is, you should always have enough respect for yourself to make sure that you're treated with respect." —Rachel

🔒

Enmeshment Is a Family Problem

This general feeling of letting others tell us how to feel is often a result of the problem of enmeshment. Family therapist Salvador Minuchin first expressed the concept of enmeshment. Enmeshment is when people are so extremely tight knit they inadvertently, or advertently, punish levels of autonomy in the system. Enmeshment involves consciously or subconsciously being told how to feel, think, and act.[1] Enmeshment may mean you're not allowed to talk with anyone outside the family about family problems. It can also be seen, for example, when you want to do something like dye your hair purple, but your parents swear they will act as if you're invisible if you do it. Maybe you're forty-six and living on your own, but you still do whatever your parents say. Or you're thirty-three and married and always check in with your family to make sure you have their permission, and blessing, to make any big choices in your life.

Enmeshment happens at any age, whether or not we are conscious of it. It can happen whether we still live at home or if our parents live on the other side of the country. And generally by the time you even realize you're enmeshed, it's hard to untangle. But it's not impossible. Even the knottiest of situations can be undone with a lot of patience and small steps of progress.

Enmeshment is usually best resolved with the help of a family therapist. This outside source can show the family where the boundaries are blurred and where the relationship is unnaturally tight. Even if you go to therapy to talk about other problems, if enmeshment is a family problem, a trained therapist will see it.

If therapy isn't an option, you'll likely have to go full steam ahead with a break up, which will be hard to do in an enmeshed family. But it may be the only option for resetting the pattern.

However you get unstuck, doing so will show you that you have the freedom to make your own choices in life.

Breaking Up with Primary Attachments

A primary attachment is the person, or people, to whom we first attached as babies. Not only are they bestowed with the all-important task of making sure you stayed alive in infancy, they are also usually the people that were in our lives on a daily basis. This primary attachment figure could be a mom or dad, grandparent, sibling, foster parent, neighbor, or any other caretaker.

For most of us in egalitarian homes, we do all right with these primary attachments. In fact, the majority of "emerging adults" (defined as adults between the ages of eighteen and twenty-nine) have a positive relationship with their parents as they mature.[2] "We've done a really good job of helping children feel cared about and understood. When that works, it works really, really, well in that many people who are raising adult children believe that they have a closer relationship with their adult children than their parents did with them at a similar age," explains Dr. Joshua Coleman, author of the book *When Parents Hurt: Compassionate Strategies When You and Your Grown Child Don't Get Along.*[3]

But, Dr. Coleman warns, the relationship can also backfire. "There's nothing that keeps adult children close to their parents at this time, beyond whether that adult child wants to be close to his or her parents. We have raised expectations about what parents should provide, but that's also a much bigger bat for a parent to be hit with later in life. In the same way that we've educated parents about child development, we're educating children about it as well. This may cause some children to be angry at their parents later in life that they didn't do more."

It wasn't until I became a mother that I really understood the sheer impossibility of being a perfect parent and I could finally grasp how easy it is to fuck parenthood up. I can see where my parents did really well and where I wish they had done things a little differently. But that doesn't mean I don't see how hard they tried. It's hard to be a parent, especially when most of us don't audition for the part and one day we just "win" the role. Even with a lot of practice, it's impossible to be perfect.

A parent being imperfect, or even strict, isn't cause for a break up. Some things that do lead to primary attachment break ups include toxicity, repetitive familial patterns, when parents go off to start second or third families, and the influence of our own spouses and partners on our relationship with parental figures.

Toxicity usually involves an abusive parent, whether it be verbal, physical, or sexual abuse; a primary attachment who exhibits danger-ous behavior, including addictions to alcohol, drugs, gambling, bring-ing random strangers home for sex, or other unacceptable acts; or a parental figure who is extremely narcissistic, controlling, or impossibly difficult to deal with. When you feel like your life is in danger or out of control because of your primary caretaker, you need to find a way to remove yourself from the situation as soon as possible for your own self-preservation.

Before you declare a relationship toxic, you need to make sure it actually is (see Chapter Three for what makes a relationship toxic). "There are genuinely toxic relationships, and there are relationships that aren't comfortable because they can be filled with conflict, even in healthy homes. On the other hand, the more difficult or troubled your parent is, the more uncomfortable it's going to be," explains Dr. Coleman.

When our parents move on to make a new life, it's hard not to feel like they're throwing out the old one too. A new family can make us feel invisible, or like a stranger with our own parental figures. In order to not feel left out, parents, stepparents, and children have to work hard to keep the family together.

Shona Vann, a journalist who also goes by the name Shona Sibary, explained her own split from her parents in the *Daily Mail* in 2011. After her father moved to Fiji to be with his new wife and stepchild, her mother left England for Canada with her third husband. "In cases like mine, it often takes years of heartbreak and a growing sense of isolation before finally [realizing] that the mother and father you once thought you knew no longer exist."[4]

If the constant reminder that a parent has moved on is too much to handle, or if you feel left behind by the new relationship, you may choose to break up with that primary attachment.

Sometimes you get your own new family and decide it's out with the old. If a primary attachment is too critical of your partner or spouse, that could isolate you from them, especially if you feel the need to protect your spouse. Or if your partner doesn't like your parent, that's an awkward situation that can potentially explode into having to choose between them.

Even if you're ready to end the relationship, your primary attachments may try hard to salvage the situation. Parents, more often than children, will take the high road when it comes to trying to keep a relationship together. When they don't, the relationship will ultimately fail. However, it's important to give your primary attachment a chance to hear what you have to say and hold on for as long as you're willing to try.

From your parent's perspective, this unconditional love may be all they have going for them in the relationship, and it may be enough to help them consider changing. While I understood the concept of unconditional love in general, I didn't grasp the concept that parents give and children receive unconditional love until the birth of my daughter. And while I may do things down the road to screw up our relationship, I will always love her with all of my heart. This is a feeling I couldn't explain as a daughter but now have no problem understanding as a parent.

♀ 🔒 ♂

Real-Life Break Ups

"My father left when I was a baby. My mother couldn't break up with her turbulent past, so instead the wrath of her storm rolled over me in the form of awful physical and mental abuse. A veritable Jekyll and Mrs. Hyde transformed day into night as she sank into yet another session of drinking that would continue until she eventually passed out. Her unconscious monstrous form would soften as the morning came, and an apparent complete loss of memory of the terrible things she had done to me the previous night had faded from her mind.

My earliest memories were conflicted between a loving mother, and an alcoholic demented demon that Satan took professional notes from.

For all the terrible things my mother did to me and to others, none of it was done when she was sober. So I loved my Mrs. Jekyll and her cooking, our trips exploring the world, and fishing off piers on little more than a shoestring. When she drank she would say that one day I would walk out on her and leave her alone in the world to die. I told her I would always stand by her, and never desert her; that I was a good son. And I believed it with all my heart.

In my later teen years I did move out to put myself through school and to work, but I made sure I was close enough to go over every weekend and help her with cleaning and gardening, and to keep her company. It was a warm Saturday afternoon when I had finished raking her leaves and had come in to get a glass of water. I saw her face and the unmistakable Jekyll looking back at me. The venom flew, but this time I ducked. I had had enough. I yelled at her, "Make a choice, me or the bottle." She looked at me with hate and told me that I didn't get to tell her what to do. I told her that if I walked out that door I would never see or speak to her again. She spat out that I was just a coward, so I did it, I walked out that door with hot tears stinging my face, and I didn't even look back.

In those brief minutes of our last face-to-face I had made a final choice that this relationship was at an end, and that I deserved better. I was not responsible for her miserable mistakes. I was not all the terrible things she told me I was. And as she had reminded me over and over through my childhood that she had sacrificed her life to bring me into the world and raise me, it did at that moment occur to me that she had it wrong. When you choose to bring a child into the world then you should be prepared to do everything in your power to give that child the best possible life you can.

After twenty-five years, I didn't see or speak to her again until her final days on Earth when I called her from the opposite side of the world to wish her a bon voyage; there was nothing else to say but that I never stopped loving her.

When I lovingly fall deep into the innocent eyes of my infant daughter, I see the simple hopes and dreams I expected for myself as a child, and all I can wish for is to not screw her life up. I know that the break up with my mother was the best decision I ever made in my life, and not just for me but for this little girl. If I could walk away from that caustic relationship and heal, then perhaps maybe, just maybe my daughter will never feel the need to break up with me." —Scott

🔒

Breaking Up with Secondary Attachments

Secondary attachments include siblings, grandparents, aunts, uncles, and cousins. Basically, these are people you aren't or have never been financially or emotionally dependent on, but whom you still call "family." Disconnection from these family members hurts because you still share memories, history, and experiences. Even distant relatives have a bond with us because we share a bloodline.

This shared history can help us grow closer as we get older, but it can also aid in creating distance. Especially when it comes to siblings or other family members we grew up with. These people have known us our whole lives, and any rivalries we had as children can be carried into our adult lives.

For example, an older sibling who beat up on her younger sister may always be seen as a bully, even after years of not bullying. It can also work this way with other negative personality traits like selfishness, bossiness, rebellion, anger, and deception. While these early personality traits often follow us into our later years, they aren't usually our primary way of relating as we get older. Still, when it comes to secondary attachments, the perceptions people have about us, and the feelings they incite, can keep us stuck in roles that aren't actually accurate any longer. It can be hard to repair the way we think, and a break up can help us reset the record playing over and over in our minds.

Fact: According to a TIME magazine article, 85 percent of adult Americans have at least one sibling, yet an estimated 3 to 10 percent have completely severed contact with them.[5]

Sometimes these relationships break up because we simply can't outrun our history. My sister and I had that problem. We were both stuck in the roles we assumed around one another as children. I was the big, bullying older sister and she was the stop-bossing-me-around younger one. Our break up, turned break, happened at a big event— our grandmother's funeral—at a time when my bossiness got the best of me.

When I tried to tell her I thought she should stay upstairs away from other people because she was sick, she said something obnoxious back to me. This brought on a short fight, the same fight we had had many times before. At the end of the three-minute altercation, I told her I didn't want to do "this" anymore. By "this," I meant get into big fights over little things.

Much to the chagrin of my parents and sister-in-law, it was the last time we spoke for over three months. She unfriended me on Facebook. But I knew that if we started talking again, it had to be different. My sister and I had gotten into this horribly ugly pattern of hating each other. She despised me for being a mean and selfish big sister, and I didn't like that she was the spoiled younger one.

After the fight at my grandmother's funeral, I began exploring what role I played in making her feel this way. I grew to understand that I wasn't a great big sister. My thoughts were always about me, not her, and I didn't care about fostering a relationship with her when we were younger.

It's been over two years since our break, and that, along with the birth of my daughter, was the best thing for our relationship. In our time apart, I could see that I was selfish, mean, and hurtful. I was truly sorry for not loving my sister better when we were both children, and I was also upset that I didn't change once I grew up and knew better. The break up gave us a chance to live in a world without one another and to see how we could shape a relationship that would work for the two of us. I don't foresee another break in our relationship; in fact, she asked me to be the maid of honor at her wedding.

Secondary attachments can break up for any number of reasons, including times of stress or death. It can happen when relatives are trying to negotiate care of an elderly primary attachment or as they're trying to figure out who gets what after they're gone. A relative not liking a new spouse can also end a relationship. So can a big move or a disagreement around running the family business.

Real-Life Break Ups

"My sister never loved me in the way that you would think sibling love would be. We loved each other because we were supposed to, but she was always extremely jealous of me—her younger sister. I have since confirmed with relatives, including my dad before he died, that she just resents the fact that I was born. When we were children, she would do anything she could to hurt and humiliate me.

Our mother died when I was twenty. My sister had a very conflicting relationship with our mom. There wasn't a lot of communication between us after that, except that every once in a while I would call her up and say, 'We're sisters. We're family. We should at least speak on the phone occasionally.' We'd go through phases where we would. She would basically talk about herself, and she would go to places where she was always manipulating the relationship.

She'd often call me in the morning even when she knew I'd been out all night. So, I said to her on the phone one day, 'I'm really, really tired right now. Can I call you back later? I can't talk.' And that's when she said to me that I was a perfect example of everything that she despised in the world. And that she wanted me to live the rest of my life as if I had no sister at all. If I tried to contact her, she said she would not respond. That was it. I remember the exact words.

I'd been through it before, so honestly I didn't think that much of it. But something clicked in me. I didn't call her back. I didn't reach out. I didn't speak with her for twenty years after that.

What I finally accepted is that my sister was never a sister to me. I think she does love me in the way that you can't help but love someone who is your sister, but she's always resented me. I should say fuck you to her, but I can't. In the bigger picture, I know there is something horribly wrong with her, and I need to figure out at what point is she responsible for her actions?

I'm in therapy where I learned it's okay to be angry. It's okay to see her as a monster. I learned to stop expecting things from her. But there's part of me that is that little girl and I really want her to love me and to be my friend. And I look at other families and sisters who are close and I don't understand why mine is different." —Amy

🔒

Options for Change

Whatever the reason, sometimes the best thing you can do for your family is take care of yourself. It may mean changing the relationship, taking a break, or breaking up. Still, it can be the greatest gift for everyone when one person has the insight and strength to walk away from a situation that isn't serving anybody at all.

FAMILY RE-BONDING

When it comes to breaking up with the most important family members of your life, including those who gave you life, you want to be really careful with the what, how, and why. Sometimes what we think is wrong in the relationship is more about not getting our way than it is about our parent's not getting it right. Only once you figure out what is really going on can you decide how to move on from a relationship that isn't working for you.

Before you close the door, answer these three questions:

1. What is the value of having this person in my life?
2. How do I feel when I'm with them?
3. What would life look like without them?

Answering these questions can help you better understand what you have to lose or gain by ending or amending the relationship.

BE CLEAR AND CONCISE

While it's easy to make a general statement, such as "You're a shitty parent," it's not going to be helpful to you or your family member to start a conversation out that way. For starters, it's not specific enough to make clear what it is about your primary attachment that upsets you. And it's defensive, trying to attack your parent before giving them a chance to explain themselves.

Even if the "shitty parent" part is true, a shitty parent won't actually be able to hear it in a productive way. Usually awful parents are awful parents for a reason. Whether they cover up their shitty with even more bad behavior (like alcohol, drugs, computer games, gambling, or being absent a lot of the time), they are wounded, damaged people who probably can't handle such harsh accusations. If you can't be gentle and non-critical, they won't hear past what a bad person they are, and they won't be able to move forward at all.

Explain to them why you feel how you feel. Give specific examples of actions that hurt you without anger or judgment. For example, "I'm having a hard time embracing you in my life because you spent so many hours at the bar when I was a child. It felt like you would rather be drinking than playing with me. I wanted you to play with me." While they still may go to the "I'm a bad parent" place, providing reasons for your hurt will help them see specific actions they have used to cover up their own pain too.

Provide them with a short explanation of your needs too. Let them know if you need some space, and thank them for listening, even if you're not sure they heard everything you said. Validating their participation in the conversation may help them understand this is a two-sided relationship, even if one side is calling the shots right now.

If you can do this face-to-face, great, but if that's tough, then try a video chat. If that's still too much, a letter is powerful too; even though it doesn't allow for an in-the-moment interaction.

CREATE RULES

While it's easy to say you're not going to participate in this relationship anymore, this is your family you're talking about. These people presumably love you as much, and sometimes more, than you love yourself.

If you want to continue working on the relationship you can write up an ultimatum in the form of a list. Clearly writing your desires down in the form of rules gives your family member one more chance to respect your boundaries. If they still can't work with the list, then you have written proof as to why the relationship isn't working.

The list should be rules for your interactions. Write everything down and read it through together. When you hand it to them, you can say something like, "I feel like our relationship continues to play out old patterns, and I want us to change some of those behaviors. I love you, and so I thought about ways we can do this. I made a list, and I'd like to share it with you and see what you think."

Or shoot them an email. You can succinctly tell them you want to find a way to improve your relationship and then send them the list of your ideas. Keep the list simple. You don't want to share fifty things your dad has to do in order to stay on your good side, but you want to make sure that it's detailed enough to highlight the changes you need to see. An example of this list might look like this:

1. Treat each other the way you'd want to be treated.
2. No yelling or screaming.
3. If a situation makes you want to yell or scream, leave until you can control your emotions and talk in a calm, cordial manner.
4. No more name-calling.
5. Offer advice only when asked.
6. Only call each other once a day—max.
7. If one of these rules is broken once, it heeds a warning. If it's broken again, we take a weeklong break. If it's broken a third time, we discuss going to therapy.

You can't change other people, but if you can stick to the changes you create, it's easier for others to want to stick to the changes too. And if this doesn't work, you can always go for the break up.

SEEK COUNSELING

You may not want to make a list or talk about your feelings one-on-one, so instead a mediator could help you through the make up or break up process. Therapists stay in business thanks to the fact that we are raised in families that operate with some level of dysfunction. All families do. It's a luxury in Western culture that we pay someone to listen to our issues with parents, siblings, aunts, uncles, cousins, or anyone else.

That being said, it's important to feel supported by people during a hard time. While friends, your spouse, or other family members may be extremely helpful, going to therapy could help even more. The best option is to go with your family member, as long as they are willing to talk about the situation with an outside person. A therapist, or mediator, can help without either family member feeling judged. He or she can also help you see both sides of your situation and find a place where you can both feel heard and happy.

Therapy is a good option for moving in the right direction. And if you're already in individual therapy and want to continue along that route, try asking your family member to agree to their own personal therapy too. This way you are both working on the situation in your own space and time.

Deciding to Break Up

Just like breaking up with your friends, there are different ways you can end the relationship with your primary and secondary attachment figures. You can meet face-to-face, do it by video chat or phone, send a letter or email, begin fading out of each other's lives, or disappear.

As always, face-to-face is the best option whenever it's emotionally and physically possible. After all, this is your family, and they do deserve to hear what you have to say to them and to see you to say good-bye. If you can't do it because of distance, then a video chat is another face-to-face option.

Sure, meeting in person may hurt a lot, but in that hurt and sadness, you will find more closure than with any other option. Of course, face-to-face comes with the pitfalls of having to deal with both sides of the issue and the possibility of a fight instead of a conversation, which then brings up the conundrum of trying to get your point across without getting defensive or frustrated.

A gentle approach is the best approach you can take with anyone you're breaking up with, especially a family member. It helps primary or secondary attachments to feel less defensive, and it may allow them to hear what you're saying, especially a parent. "For a parent, hearing that they made mistakes is very hard—no matter the person," explains Dr. Coleman. "Most parents take the job quite seriously, and even if they did a really poor job, their perception of themselves as parents will still be very central to their self-esteem and identity."

Start with the good and work your way to the bad. Tell your parent, for example, what you liked about their parenting. Tell your sibling what you enjoyed about being their sister. Share a good time you had with a cousin. This way, they don't assume the goal is to bring them down. Then, let them know, in no uncertain terms, that you're ending this relationship.

Avoid shame and humiliation. Don't character assassinate. Instead of saying "You were . . ." say, "I didn't get/feel . . ." or "I needed . . ." Or try "There are ways I felt . . ."

Say your piece, and say good-bye.

If confronting a family member brings up all sorts of angst and other issues, you can write your feelings down in a letter or an email. Make sure to explain your emotions and tell them how and where you think things went wrong. If it's a lifetime of wrong, make sure you let them know how you feel about how the relationship has evolved. Write down details of what you perceive as flaws, but again, find a way to do this that won't make them feel like they are all evil and you are all good.

When it comes to writing letters, it's not always easy to make sure your words have been received (both on a physical level and an emotional one). You may want to send the letter both in electronic form and written form, upping the odds of successful delivery. If you have the option of read receipt, like delivery confirmation, you can use that too.

Real-Life Break Ups

"I wish I had been able to do the cold turkey thing with my dad because from the outside it looks easier. And it feels easier than struggling back and forth between knowing what is the right thing to do. But I also know that if you can shut somebody off like that, what else are you shutting off? You probably never dealt with why you shut the person off. And when you're done, you don't have to think about it again. Where I'm probably spending too much time thinking about it. I'd like to be somewhere in between. God knows what you can accomplish in therapy." —Tracie

Dealing with the Rest of Your Family

The other members of your family may not understand your decision to end things with the other relative. Or they may totally get it, having had similar experiences to you, but they may not be ready or have the drive or desire to completely end their relationship with your parent, uncle, or cousin. (On the flip side, your break up could be impetus for their break up too.)

Your family members may feel annoyed by your break up, whether because you upset the familial balance or because they now have to deal with the relative in question to help them get through this ending. A family member may go to extremes to let you know just how much your break up has hurt the family unit. They may pester you to make things work or cut you off so they can prove to you that you can be hurt too. They may deliver messages from the broken up relative or bug you with calls and texts. They could post happy family photos on social media (or send them via email) so you can see what you're missing out on. The best option is to block them from your news feed or ignore their emails, if this happens.

You may get criticism from the rest of your family for any number of things, including giving your family member an ultimatum and telling them that if they don't change, they are being cut out of your life. You may be criticized for not telling them they need to change and cutting them out of your life anyway. You may be called cruel or heartless because you wrote a letter instead of dealing with the family member face-to-face, or some members of your clan may snub you because you broke up with another member of the tribe. And since this is family, you can't run away from them all (at least not in most situations). And even if you can, who are you really hurting in that instance? (Answer: yourself.)

♀ 🔒 ♂

Real-Life Break Ups

"My dad was born in a detention camp around Germany right after World War II. He moved to New York early on, and eventually became a police officer. When I was eleven, I asked my mother if she and my dad were in love. My mom gave me some roundabout answer that basically amounted to no. My mom and I would literally sit in the living room while my dad was at work and pray for him to be shot in the line of duty.

I learned a little later on that the reason my mom would never leave him was that he threatened to kill her if she ever tried. With him being in the police force, he had her convinced that there was no way she could have him arrested.

My mother did leave eventually. During the divorce, I kept talking to my dad so that he would think everything was fine. My mom moved in with me for a while, and my sister and I both stopped talking with my dad after the divorce was final. It wasn't even a question. My dad reached out to me a few months later. I wrote him a four-page email and asked him to answer some specific questions that I needed answered. He didn't answer any of the questions. He told me that he had problems writing and would rather talk. I insisted that he needed to answer these questions before we spoke. I haven't heard from him since. I gave him three tries and that was it. That was 2005.

My sister was born seven years after me, so we weren't especially close. She has very similar attributes to my father, including anger issues. She didn't have a lot of friends after high school or college. She wrote off friends. Held grudges.

I always got the impression that my sister could do without me. The final straw was when she wouldn't pick me up at the airport, even though I tried to fly in at a convenient time for her and her husband.

That was the end.

I don't like holding grudges, but for me it was always about improving my life. With my father it was for past transgressions. With my sister it's like why would I subject myself to her current abuse? Part of me thinks that if I reach out to them, especially my dad, that he won. I have more pride than that. It's sad because there's a lot to be said about forgiveness, but I guess I could do both, forgive my father and sister but not carry on the relationship with them." —Ryan

Family relationships might be uncomfortable, but sometimes there are conditions that come along with the break up. And these "sacrifices" can be worth the discomfort of having to deal with the ex-family member every once in a while. Especially if you're bearing the discomfort for someone you really care about. For example, if your ninety-year-old grandmother cherishes the fact that she can have all the girls come together every month for a visit, then you can grin and bear that one day a month with your "evil" stepmother. Or if your sister is getting married and she still talks to your dad but you don't, you can find a way to make her big day about her and not a big deal for you.

It isn't your decision if your child wants to have a relationship with a grandparent that you can no longer stand to be around. Maybe there's another family member who can act as a go-between to make sure your child gets to have the grandparent experience. Or maybe you can act cordial long enough for a drop-off and pick-up. When the relationship isn't about you but you have to be involved, it can mean a lot to others for you to suck it up sometimes.

Whatever happens, if a family member tries to talk you out of the break up, here are some things you can say to them:

1. I love you. This isn't about you, and I prefer to not make it about us.
2. I'm willing to talk about this with you, as long as there is no blame or accusation.
3. I have to do this for myself. It's not my intention to hurt you in the process.
4. This is my experience.
5. I'm willing to give you the space you need to process this situation, and I'm open to talking this through with you when you are ready to accept my decision.

The best way to deal with family is to deal with yourself first. Start by observing how you react to your family's accusations or insistence that you and your attachment find a way to end this "silly fight." Once you have the self-awareness to understand your reactions, you can determine if and how your emotions played a role in the break up. You may also want to find a way to remain grounded. Going to the gym, practicing yoga, or meditating are all ways that can help you stay level-headed during a time when you may feel anything but. Keeping a journal during the break up process can help you get a better sense of how you were feeling throughout the experience and give you a chance to continue to monitor your feelings and thoughts.

Truth is, you may feel relief, joy, or excitement around the end of a relationship that has caused you a lifetime of pain, frustration, fear, or anger. And if that's the place you get to, great. But a lot of times when it comes to familial break ups, it's a sad, hard place—especially once you realize what you thought was a forever is instead no more.

CONSIDERATIONS FOR THE BROKEN UP

For this chapter, I interviewed Dr. Joshua Coleman, parental estrangement expert and author of the book *When Parents Hurt: Compassionate Strategies When You and Your Grown Child Don't Get Along*. Although his advice is geared towards a split between children and their primary attachment figures, it can be used in any familial break up.

1. Adult children sometimes need or want space for their own growth and change. Sometimes they just need to feel separate. Either way, giving your child space could be very useful to their development.

2. Be respectful. Listen and be interested in what your child has to say. If you can see their desire for change as a growth opportunity, you have the potential to be closer down the road.

3. If your family member ends contact with you, express empathy. Tell them, "It's clear that you need this, and I don't want you to feel guilty about it. I know you wouldn't do this unless you felt like it was in your best interest to do so. When you're ready to have contact, I'll be here, and the door will always be open. If there are things I haven't addressed yet, regarding your hurt and what you're upset about, please let me know."

4. Embrace the kernel of truth that there is something there you need to address.

5. You can stop trying to reconnect with your child, as long as the child isn't a minor. If the child is a minor, you should continue to reach out because you have to assume that they may be operating under forces that are bigger than them.

SEVEN

Kissing Community
Goodbye

When professor and sociologist Charles Josiah (C. J.) Galpin first coined the term "community" in 1915, I bet he never imagined just how the definition would expand (his original definition referred to the social anatomy of a rural community).[1] Now there are so many different types of communities, big and small, sleepy and strange. Take, for instance, the community of Gibsonton ("Gibtown"), Florida—a town that was once known for its retired freak show performers, including "Lobster Boy," "Al the Giant," and "Jeanie the Half Girl."

Or Cairo's "Garbage City" at the far end of Manshiyat Naser. The community is known as Cairo's largest collective of garbage collectors, and yeah, that's what they do. And you don't have to go across the ocean to visit our very own Slab City in Southern California (a post-apocalyptic community of artistic proportions).

I love being a part of community. I belong to sex educator communities like the San Francisco Sex Information and the American

Association of Sex Educators Counselors and Therapists (AASECT).
I'm also part of a community of people who make a pilgrimage to the
desert once a year to spend a few weeks together building a city so they
can burn it all down in a few glorious nights. It's called Burning Man,
and the people in the community are known as "Burners," and really
it's about so much more than just what is built and burned. There are
new-mom communities and communities of people who hike together
or bike together that I also enjoy dabbling in.

Of course, community can refer to a specific geographical location. For example, all people who live in the Santa Cruz mountains are
a part of the same community. Or community can refer to a group of
people who all live in a particular building or complex, like a senior
home or a development of houses that all are accessed through the
same gated road. It can be a town, a county, a country, or a universe.
Community can refer to people at your University with whom you
share the same major or who happen to be in your same dormitory. It
can refer to a sorority or a fraternity or any other group you join where
the interests of the group keep everybody together.

Community may be about religion, about attending the same
church, temple, or mosque. It may have to do with what god you believe
in or what god you don't believe in. It may be about the color of your
skin or the generation in which you were born.

It may be about shared goals, like Alcoholics Anonymous, a community for supporting people who need or want to stay away from alcohol. It can also be social, for example, a group of fetishists who all like
to dress up as clowns may be part of a clown play community. People
who proudly don their red hat and purple clothing may be showing off
membership in the community known as the Red Hat Society.

Community can also go dark, as in secret societies and places
where one worships a leader or belief that is very much alive. It may
take on a cultlike appearance, one in which thought manipulation is
part of the process. Membership may come easily in these situations,
but once you're in, you can feel like there's no way out.

The Value of Community

Community is a collective group of people who we believe in and who have our back. We often see or think of community as "our people," because we share a common area of interest or a common goal with this particular group. Oftentimes these people help us strengthen our identities; allow us to share in a united goal or interest; and lift us up and allow us to feel safe, supported, and well cared for. That means that when the going gets tough, community helps us stay strong. If we look at members of a community individually, we may refer to them as friends, brothers, sisters, or another intimate label that identifies them as close to our heart. As a group collective, they are so much more than that. When we are sick, they come together to make us well by delivering food, taking us to doctor appointments, and staying with us when we don't want to be alone. When we need financial help, they rally to raise money for the cause. When we need a place to throw a party, they use their resources to help us find a space.

Communities place values on their members, just as members place value on their communities. Community can evoke feelings of commitment, fellowship, mutuality, independence, belonging, interdependence, connection, and empowerment. Community shows us the way to balance independence with collaboration. You may have felt like an outsider in your family of origin, your school, or even your body. But when you find your community, it can feel like you have found home—a place where you are understood and accepted.

On the flip side, community can be a source of codependence, making us feel isolated from the rest of the world and even becoming our only source of information and warping our values. It can make us doubt ourselves as individuals. And when that happens, community starts to fail.

Still, we expect community to help us shine. We use it to lift our spirits, feel a shared connection, show and reflect support, help us grow, challenge our thinking, and allow us to experience a plethora of love and kindness. When the connection becomes disconnection, we can feel disoriented, alone, and completely destroyed. When our community can no longer support our beliefs, ideas, and experiences, we can feel so lost that we may search a long time to find another positive outlet for support.

Community is bigger than we are. It's bigger than family, friends, and coworkers. It may be the biggest concept we can attach to on this planet. And when something big comes crashing down, it can leave us feeling so small and insignificant that we aren't sure where to go next.

Breaking up with community can be tough. But staying in a community that isn't working for you is tougher.

Breaking Up with a Religious or Spiritual Community

❝ *I left the church. I mumbled something about people chang-ing, about needing different things, about needing to be apart in order to be together someday, about needing to reclaim ourselves as individuals so we didn't die on the inside or end up hating and resenting each other. I wanted God to stop me from leaving. I wanted God to promise things would be different. I wanted God to beg me to come back. But God didn't say a word. So I broke up with God. I wasn't gentle. 'It's not me,' I said. 'It's you.'* **❞**

—SARAH SENTILLES, AUTHOR, *BREAKING UP WITH GOD*[2]

If you have a religious affiliation, especially if you were born into it, sooner or later, you will most likely challenge something that religion says or does. Whatever it is, there will be a time in your life when you question your involvement in your religion for any number of reasons: for its purpose in your life, for its social and political views, for its exclu-sionary or inclusionary ways, or for its cost on your time or your wallet.

While you will be encouraged to work through your doubts by lean-ing on your community to find support and answers, it's your individual decision to figure out just what God, or any other entity, means to you.

And if you can work through your doubts and this makes you feel better able to continue on the path with your religious organization, then good for you. But if you feel that it's time to seek out some or no other spirituality, you will likely go through a process of reflection and rejection.

When it's time to decide if you are going to lose your religion, religious influences will be all up in your spirit, trying to make it more difficult to come to a decision that doesn't involve sticking it out. You may be subject to scare tactics trying to be passed off as truths. You may be told it's not Christ-like, Buddha-esque, mindful, or in God's plan for you to go your separate way. You may hear that when you walk away from God, you lose your place in heaven (a belief you may or may not choose to stick with anyway), or that a devout member sticks with their faith through the good times and bad. A break up with your religion is a highly charged and often extremely challenging decision to make.

> **Fact:** *According to the Pew Research Center, one-fifth of the U.S. population doesn't have a religious affiliation. This includes 13 million self-described atheists and agnostics and nearly 33 million other people who opt out of choosing any particular religious affiliation.*[3]

You're Ending a Committed Relationship

Not only does breaking up with your religion disconnect you from a belief, but it may also disconnect you from the people who hold those beliefs. It means people who only see things through the lens of religion may not be able to see you anymore. Your religious family and friends may feel like you are testing their ability to believe. Or they may doubt your ability to understand them any longer. Either way, a break in religion can create a rift in your community and in your family too, if they are also invested in this religion. There will be some members who believe you should put your church above yourself. Their words will make you doubt your own feelings and thoughts, but it is your gut that gives you the strongest indication of what is working for you and what isn't. So go with it.

Other times, breaking up with a religion doesn't mean you have to break up with everyone in the religion. In a recent episode of MTV's *True Life*, Nathan, a pastor's son, leaves his Christian church, but not his Christian family, to study Buddhism.

Happy ending or not, time does heal. Leaving your church or other religious affiliation may feel like leaving a marriage, and in a sense, it is. You've created a union, a commitment with God, Buddha, or Krishna. And now you are breaking that vow. When you leave a religion, you may feel a sense of emptiness and a sense of fear about the future. These are fixable things. By filling your life with a support person or group, new interests, activities, and friends that engage your spirit and your brain, you will pave a new path for your next long-term religious relationship. You will be able to commit again, but it will be a new and informed commitment. And that's a pretty great feeling.

FIND OBJECTIVE SUPPORT

Whenever you make a big decision, you don't need to do it alone. To figure out what exactly you're going to do and how you're going to do it, find someone who understands your community and can also stay objective as you explain your ideas and feelings to them. You need the kind of person who promises to keep an open mind, listen with compassion, and accept whatever decision you make. This may be a friend who isn't a member but knows what the church means to you. Or it may be a therapist or other spiritual advisor. Don't share far and wide yet. Wait to tell those who are going to try to convince you otherwise until you have actually made your decision.

THE NAUGHTY-AND-NICE LIST

Make a list of the pros and cons of staying and leaving. Have that list handy when you talk with your friend or former church members. This shows you've really thought your decision through, and it lets everybody know that you are making a well-considered choice.

SAY IT IN A LETTER

Sometimes the easiest way to say good-bye to a large group of people is through a letter. While you don't have to explain in detail what you're doing (at least not in all churches), it is a nice gesture to let them know that you are taking a break from your beliefs. Thank them for their time. If you want to get specific, by all means express your reasons for leaving. If it's a matter of values, let them know what you don't agree with so that they can possibly rethink these issues in the future. If it's that you feel you are being called to find spirituality elsewhere, let them know so they can leave you to find your path. The church will likely want you back, but that will be your choice to make.

ASK FOR AN EXIT INTERVIEW

If you feel you owe the church more than a handwritten good-bye, because of how active you were or because it's the highest road you can take, then by all means ask for an exit interview. However, don't expect the exit to be easy. While you may do everything right and feel good about saying good-bye, it can also go south, especially if they feel like they are being judged. Nobody likes when you believe their ideas are wrong, but some may envy you for having the courage to stand up for what you believe.

Most importantly, be confident in your choice and stand strong in your conviction. If you stay strong, you will come through the other end with a feeling of liberation that you will enjoy. Try repeating the mantra "My reasons are valid and legitimate" every time you have doubts.

After Cutting the Cord

Once you've said what you needed to say, it's time to sever all ties with the church. If you still have friends or family actively involved in your former religious affiliation, you may want to have a discussion with them about the boundaries of talking about religion with you. Perhaps you put a moratorium on discussions about spiritual beliefs for the next twelve months, and when the wounds have healed a bit, you can see if it's still too soon to bring things up. If conversations do arise, have a plan of action in place to get the heck out of them. A simple "excuse me" before you leave the room could work to get the message across.

If it feels like a big deal that you left your coven, then it is. So use this separation to allow you to find your separate sense of self. Be sure to make new friends, or at least make time for new things in your life. While you may or may not keep your old friends, take some space from them. It's important to be able to establish a sense of individualism before you try to reconnect with even a part of what once was your whole community. Look for new people who challenge you to open up and explore what it is you are seeking.

In your search, you may decide you need a new outlet for self-reflection, perhaps something that you consider deeply spiritual. Meditation and yoga work for some and can keep you connected to your body and a higher spiritual calling. A new ritual may replace your old religion too. Joining a singing group can provide you with a place to let the spirit move through you. So can a Five Rhythms dance group, which is a community of people who come together to transcend through dance and movement. You can also volunteer your time with Big Brothers Big Sisters of America or some other organization that helps you feel like you are serving a higher purpose. Another religion may help you fill the void your old religion left. Of course, you don't have to close the door to your church, temple, or coven forever. But you do have to be open to finding your own path, so you can come to your own inner truth in your time.

♦ ▪ ♦

Real-Life Break Ups

"My mother grew up Southern Baptist in a small town. It was the kind of town that had two or three churches for denomination differences.

I did not grow up in that town, but on major holidays and random visits I was obligated to attend service at that church. I attended Bible school regularly, and I even went to Summer Bible Camp. At one point—around the age of twelve or thirteen—I had thoughts of becoming a minister, but I could never wrap my mind around it because my denomination believed that women could not lead a congregation.

What I loved about my religion was the absolute conviction that all suffering and pain was for a reason and reward was simply around the corner. And I *loved* how amazing the world sounded through a Southern Baptist sermon. Hellfire and brimstone was often followed by celebration and gratitude for the grace of God.

But I left Christianity, Southern Baptist specifically, because of sex. After I had my first orgasm with a partner, I spent two hours crying because I had broken some sort of vow to God. I tend to dislike anything that makes me dislike me. So I decided I needed to figure out if I was really willing to abstain or if I needed to rethink my beliefs. For a while I continued with my sexual escapades, convinced that the Old Testament was just outdated, and that this was fine. But then, I made my first friend who was homosexual. And my religion said that was not acceptable. My mom said that homosexuality is natural (as all things are created by God, including sin); however, it is our job as moral and Christian people to abstain from 'sins of the flesh.' And that was that for me. The concept that people should just walk around abstaining from their natural urges didn't seem right to me. So I could not reconcile all of this in my head. Add that to the fact that my youth minister apparently cheated on his wife and had to make a public announcement during Sunday service as an apology to the church for false ministry, and I was gone.

I left quietly. I was a teenager, and most teenagers didn't go to church often. About two years after that, I decided I was done with the religion completely, and then I told my mom. My mom cried and said, 'It makes me sad that when I die and meet my savior, none of my family will be there.' My father is not a religious man. He was disfellowshipped from the Kingdom Hall of Jehovah's Witnesses.

Throughout this process, I learned to acknowledge that true acceptance means accepting beliefs that are both more conservative and less. I still find faith beautiful and have very good friends who are also devout ones. I occasionally envy them." —April

● ● ●

"I grew up in the Mormon Church—by choice. I loved everything I knew about our religion, and each Sunday I would take the bus to church where I would stand behind the pulpit and bare my testimony that this was the one true church. I would sing and eat the blood or body of Christ from a silver tray. The seemingly infallible Elders in their crisp white shirts with perfectly placed name tags were my true heroes, and I yearned to one day follow in their footsteps. The LDS (Latter Day Saints) represented everything good in the world, and much of who I am today stems from what I learned within the church's sunlit walls.

The seeds of doubt started to grow inside me one day when I was standing in the hall of my church. Two men who I greatly respected were having a conversation; one said to the other, 'Evolution is ridiculous, to imagine that man comes from apes is stupid. How can anybody believe in evolution and God at the same time?' The conversation went on, but I was already lost in deep thought. I believed in both God and evolution but had never considered that they were diametrically opposed. What a conundrum I now faced at the age of thirteen. I was taught that in order to love God, one must truly accept his existence into one's heart, and since I was committed to the theory of evolution, that meant I couldn't believe in him too. For years after that I held onto the bare threads of my faith, but like a rock climber suspended from a faulty rope, I was simply waiting for the last strand to snap (and hoping the rope might just save me). I remained suspended from that rope for twenty more years, but it just kept unraveling.

The rope finally broke when I learned the church actively worked to deny same-sex marriage. To deny not just the relationships of members of my family, but also of friends I adored. How could anybody deny the love and rights of these people who had committed to each other and demonstrated the very best of what we as humans can be?

The last time I ever walked into my church was to deliver a detailed ten-page letter to the Deacons' office to say good-bye and explain why. Not to debate with anybody, but to give them a written legacy to ponder and perhaps learn from. They had lost me forever, and that should be their tragedy, their sin.

Despite all the good that the church had given me, the bad was not only insufferable but was contradictory to what the church had taught me. Racism, prejudice, greed, hypocrisy, disrespect, hate, and ignorance are the true enemy of humanity, spirit, and the heart, and no god or religion would or should deny this." —Scott

●●●

"My family has been Jehovah's Witnesses (on both sides) for four generations. I was a Jehovah's Witness from the time I was born until I was twenty-seven. I loved the camaraderie, and the sense that everyone was your family.

I left because something was wrong in my life, I didn't know what, so I left everything—my husband, the church, my job. I didn't go back because I learned about the lies those in charge perpetuated regarding doctrine.

The Jehovah's Witnesses have what they call Judicial Committees (JC), where you confess your 'sin' and they decide if you should be 'disfellowshipped' or not. When trying to return to the church, they also decide if you're repentant enough to be 'reinstated.' I basically turned myself in to the elders because I felt like I wasn't worthy and I deserved God's punishment by being disfellowshipped. I told my parents face-to-face that I was being disfellowshipped from the congregation after my JC but before the official announcement was made to the congregation.

Now, no one in the church is allowed to associate with me. My parents occasionally speak to me, but really only in regards to my children. My biological brothers don't speak to me at all. Not one of my 'friends' stayed in contact with me, beyond those who also left the church.

When I left, I didn't trust people in general, and I was still in shock from all the changes in my life at the time. It started with one person, who dragged me into her family. It took years to build friendships with those I now consider part of my 'tribe.'

I learned everything about myself after leaving. When you're a Jehovah's Witness, you're told what to think, how to act, what to wear, who to talk to, and what you're allowed to watch and listen to. It's conform or leave. Appearances are *everything* to them. Most live double lives. When you find out your entire life has been a lie, you start at the bedrock and rebuild. Therapy saved my sanity. Mostly I learned that I get to make my own life rules; I don't have to follow what society says or what some religious person says. I am in charge of my own morality, and I'm not responsible for anyone else." —Janet

🔒

How to Break Up with a Cult

The word *cult* was originally used to describe various religious practices, but now it mainly refers to small, independent sects who hold more eccentric beliefs. Cults are generally devoted to a particular person, object, or idea. Some people see any religion as a cult, but cults are often more extreme versions of religions—exploiting members both psychologically and sometimes financially through psychological manipulation. Cults demand you prove your loyalty and make you obey their leader. Some cults, like Heaven's Gate and the Peoples Temple Agricultural Project (known as Jonestown), expect you to devote your life (and death) to their ideas.

Cults are often unhealthy, making you anxious and dependent, although at the right time and place, some people use cults as a healthy way to gain insight into various aspects of their own lives. I have at times been involved in cults—not the scary kind that ask for your life, just the kind that ask for your money and your mouth (to spread the word that they exist and do good). I like cults because I learn something about myself every time I am exposed to one, but I am also certain that I will always leave (and I always have). But when you are told you can't leave even if you want to, then you know you have to get out.

Thought reform, a type of mind control, is a powerful tool to keep members from questioning life outside of the community. Controlling your mind makes it easy to control your movements. You become a human puppet being pulled by the strings of a leader.

When people leave extreme cults, it's important they consult with a professional who is trained in cult deprogramming. They can help you deal with post traumatic stress disorder and self-esteem issues. Whatever thoughts you have about leaving a cult, it isn't easy, and there are online and in-person resources that can help you get to a better place.

❝ *If you try to confront someone directly who is in something like [a cult], you are just going to push them further away. What always worked for me was when people didn't act shocked. I used to work at McDonald's and I would tell the people I worked with about 'The Lord,' and they would react with an, 'Oh, okay, that's cool. That's nice. So what are you doing Friday night? We're having a bonfire party. We'd love if you came.' Instead of trying to talk somebody out of it, presenting them with a more appealing option could be the way to reach someone.* **❞**

—SARAH, FORMER CULT MEMBER

Go Outside Yourself

Because leaving a cult challenges your sense of community and your sense of self, you want to find some outside help, whether it's other family or friends or people you meet online who have had similar experiences. The International Cultic Studies Association (ICSA) is a leading organization for helping those who want to break up with "physically manipulative high control groups," and they have been offering support and services since 1979 (www.icsahome.com).

If you have the option, make a careful list of people you want to talk to, and then start reaching out to see if they're available to help. Don't turn to anyone who may slip up and share your secret before you're ready to make it public. You may want to talk to a therapist or someone who's been friendly to you every time you go to the grocery store (especially if you have no other options). You should also consider putting some solid legal counsel on the list (just in case). Go to the doctor and get a check up of the physical and mental kind. Plan out where you'll live after you leave. If you had your own home, is it still safe to be there?

Getting Out

It may be difficult to leave a cult with a face-to-face ending. While it's still the boldest way to go, it can also backfire. Instead of telling the whole group, try telling one member of the group. Meet in a neutral, public place where you can break the news to them and still feel safe. If you want backup, bring a friend with you. Then let the member go back and tell the rest of the group.

You can also try a phone call or sending a letter. Either of these options lets you write out, in detail, what you want to say while leaving some distance between you and the community you need to say it too. With a letter, they can choose to read it out loud to the whole group so everybody knows exactly how you're feeling or to keep it amongst the leaders.

If you choose a phone call, write down the specifics of what you want to say, and stick to your points. If you are afraid to make the

ADVICE ON BREAKING UP
FROM FORMER CULT MEMBER

Paul Grosswald, a former cult member turned lawyer specializing in cult litigation, offers tips on leaving a cult:

"Instinct is awareness. Being in a cult taught me to suppress my doubts so that I would think there was something wrong with me and not the organization. That's how they got me to overlook the bad stuff. That's a dangerous attitude. If you're questioning something about your community, trust your instincts. Questioning means that something is wrong.

Mind control and suppression are forms of abuse. The cult was treating me like crap, but I was determined to work my way back into it. I deflected the blame away from them and onto my parents (who were, at the time, trying to actively get me out).

Get help. I don't know that I could have talked myself through that process without a counselor. Find other experts and counselors, and not just any counselor, but an exit counselor who really understands the mechanisms of a cult. Exit counselors can be anyone doing an intervention to get somebody out of a cult. This is someone who can show you that your reasoning is flawed and there is another perspective and another way of looking at life. You may find one through a cult recovery network (http://www.culteducation.com/directory.html) or through word of mouth. You need to free yourself from the ideology, and that's something that can be virtually impossible to do without knowledgeable support.[4]"

phone call directly, you can have an outside family member or friend (or whoever you have turned to for support) make the call for you. They can deliver your message and provide you with the distance you need to make a break from everyone else.

Breaking up is hard. While disappearing isn't the best way to end most relationships, it may be the best option in this situation—especially if you are already scared about leaving the community. Still, you'll want to use an exit counselor to help you get out and stay out.

Because cult members will likely try to win you back, you will need to keep your distance. You don't have to answer their emails or phone calls, but if you do, write a short message asking them to never contact you again. Or again, you can have a friend write the message for you.

Keep a record of all the times they try to contact you and of your responses. Harassment laws do exist in every country, and it may surprise you to find out what kind of protection you are entitled to.

Eventually, you will replace your cult with other, more positive groups. Where you go and who you choose will be a conscious choice because you will again be in control of your life.

♦ 🔒 ♦

Real-Life Break Ups

"My parents found Brother Julius in 1970, when they were doing a lot of spiritual searching, and they heard about this guy who was giving baptisms and claiming to be John the Baptist reincarnated. This was before he decided he was Jesus reincarnated. So they got involved in his cult, and I was born into it. No choice. Similar to David Koresh's teachings, Brother Julius was a sinful messiah. He was overweight and imperfect, but it was all for a divine reason.

I was in the cult until I was twenty, when I got kicked out. I was just pushing boundaries constantly and never could really fit in; despite the fact that I believed that Brother Julius was God, I was always misbehaving. I couldn't help myself.

So, I got called in to a spiritual consultation, and when I showed up, I didn't bring my Bible, which was a big no-no. Everyone worships their Bibles and carries them around. I had been at work all day and forgot mine, so that was the first problem. They had collected a lot of information on me, so they knew what I had been doing, who I had been associating with, and none of it was acceptable. I was holding hands. Kissing boys that were in the church and not in the church. So I got kicked out.

I never got to have the confrontation I wanted, which would have been great if I had been strong enough to do that, but I don't know if I would have ever been able to do that. So it was probably good for me that it happened the way it happened. Otherwise, I probably would have been contrite for a while and then maybe had just gone back whenever they were ready to talk to me again. At some point they would have let me back in. But my leaving helped my cousin leave too. Because she thought I did it on my own, she felt empowered to do it too. And I'm really happy about that." —Sarah

● ● ●

"I left my church. I did not want to be psychologically manipulated, and I did not want to be exploited, psychologically or financially. They sometimes said from the pulpit, 'You are free to go. The doors are all unlocked.' While that was true, they also knew there were psychological reasons people would not 'need' to be locked in.

So I walked away. I avoided the barrage of leaders trying to 'get together' with me to manipulate me, and I reached out to friends who had been excommunicated for support. After a few weeks, the leaders grew tired of calling and trying to set up meetings with me when I refused to respond. I did a lot of writing, reading, thinking. I found a social worker, went to the doctor, tried new hobbies, and reached out to people I lost contact with because of the cult.

I didn't really document my decompression out of the church. I used the Internet, but YouTube (where I have my own videos about leaving) was not around during the time I left. Instead, I was finding things like the Apathetic Agnostic Church of Atheism. So, it's really interesting now that you have all kinds of information online for deconverting.

Particularly interesting to me is the idea of coming out of the church and not really having a good concept of what the real world is like. Because when you are a part of the church, it's such an insular community. There's so much anxious dependency. There's this idea that when you leave the church, you're going to leave this community. I was fortunate enough to leave the church with a husband who was skeptical by nature and who really loved me when we left. That's not a given. There's so much control of every aspect in your life, it's hard to be in a setting without those particular scripts in your mind." —Lisa

● ● ●

"I broke up with a group of spiritual trainers. They like to think of themselves as the Harvard of metaphysics. I truly felt I had found my path, my purpose in life, until I finally realized that it was a top-down pyramid scheme. They charge thousands of dollars for healings and workshops to be 'certified' in certain healings.

Once that happened, I just stopped talking to everyone. For weeks I received phone calls from members trying to entice me back, telling me my negative ego was getting in the way. I eventually had to just ignore the calls, and I stopped going to events that I knew members would be at.

I really missed the feeling of community, the intense 'energy highs,' and feeling like I had a higher purpose. So, for a long time I drank heavily. I even went on anti-depressants for a while. I felt that my self was fragmented and I didn't know who I was or what reality was anymore. I finally reconciled with my friends, who thought I was crazy for joining the group in the first place, and I got back into yoga, hiking, and rock climbing. Being active has really helped.

I learned that you are your own guru, and you are the only one that can save yourself. I learned that I don't need to search for a 'higher purpose.' I just need to seek the things that make me feel alive, and everything else will come together." —Ciara

🔒

Breaking Up with Social Media

Social media has changed our way of interacting with family and friends and has blown wide open the definition of what it means to have a community (and followers). For starters, friends aren't always people we have met in the flesh, and followers don't necessarily refer to people who live and breathe our every word. Nowadays we can live a seemingly full life (whether it's fulfilling or not) in the virtual realm.

We share a lot of ourselves, including our thoughts and fears, our hopes and dreams, and pictures of what we are eating for breakfast, lunch, and dinner with our social media connections. We ask for help, forgiveness, and advice on the Web. I got people to share their real break up stories thanks to social media. While social media can be a wonderful connection for us, it can also waste of a lot of our time. It can destroy relationships because we misinterpret what someone wrote or we get annoyed with the views that someone has or because they're actually writing to someone behind our back. And while most people wouldn't romantically break up on social media (even if they break up over it), we end relationships with all sorts of people—especially "friends"—on the very same site we may have connected. Especially when those friends say something we deem really offensive (like a racist comment) or because we're sick of seeing their posts on their love for Jesus or the Tea Party. And sometimes we break up with social media too.

When we find that we've devoted an entire twenty-four hours to living on our screen, we may realize that social media is sucking away too much of our life. We may make the decision to end our time online so we can go be in life. Most of the time, this break is temporary, which makes it all the more important to share our leave of absence with the rest of our virtual world.

Before you delete your profile from any of a number of sites, send out a last post, tweet, picture, or message letting your community know that you are taking a break. Because we don't always stay up to date on all of our friends at any given moment, leaving without the final message can seem like a big deal to any number of people. They may think it's just them you're breaking up with.

When taking a break, find a way to break the news to your circle.

HOW DO YOU BREAK UP
WITH SOCIAL MEDIA?

"I have had to take a few breaks from Facebook. I simply write a post the day before so that people have a heads up. It is a terrible addiction, this Facebook world, and I have always come back. The hardest part is that I live two thousand miles away from my hometown, so this is my connection to them."

"I have just deleted my account [in the past]. I was off for about five months. I didn't say anything to anyone. Just hit delete. And I never went back to that account. I have no idea where all the stuff from that account is now."

"A couple of years ago I was really grief stricken and I needed to take myself off Facebook for a month. I did not want to read any more bad news. I told everyone I was taking a leave of absence and that one day I would be back."

"Every year I take a break for Lent. I find it gives me time to evaluate how social media affects my life. I use the time to rediscover my surroundings, physically connect with friends and family, create a new recipe, find a new crochet stitch to master, and reflect on my many blessings."

If nothing else, it's a common courtesy and a way to make sure that no one tries to send you an important message while you're away.

Breaking Up with Other Communities

Physical groups of people who organize under a common interest or goal have been around a lot longer than social media ones. They aren't as drastic in their rules and regulations as other, cult like organizations. These communities of interest don't require you to drink the Kool-Aid, although some of them may like you better when you do. These can be communities you meet through organized festival groups like Burning Man, sororities and fraternities, or your local writers group. You usually leave them because you outgrow the purpose they serve in your life. It may just be that you no longer want to do "that" or be "this."

When I was in college, I pledged a sorority. I pledged an incredible, fun, smart sorority, and yet it was the idea of sororities that I chose to leave. I did get a lot out of my sorority in terms of friendship. Some of my closest friends from college are women I once referred to as "sister.".

Beyond the friendships, and at first the social life pledging afforded me, I grew weary of members-only groups. So, after a semester abroad in Australia, I decided to come back home to a more independent college experience. I had this righteous thought in my mind that voting on people was now mean, cruel, and uncaring and that I didn't want to be responsible for other girls feeling rejected too.

I only left after the president, who happened to be my little sister, asked me to (since I refused to vote). I still kept the friends I had made in the community, but I left the experience of being associated with those three Greek letters. Looking back, I wish I had addressed the group with a more formal good-bye and let them know my feelings, so that they could understand me and not form their own opinions based on other people's stories about what happened. But that's not how it went down. Live and learn.

Odds are, you have made some friends with common interests by being a member of a group. And while you may break up with the community at large, you may like being friends with some of the group's members. In this type of break up, you may feel more left out by the collective even if you remain in contact with some of its members. Staying in touch with some people may also leave you struggling to establish an identity that is separate from the group you just left. If you don't make a clean break, you'll want to set some boundaries with those people you choose to stay in touch with. For example, keep talk about the community off-limits. After all, if that's all you really have in common, how far can the relationship go?

You can also get together on a set day and time with a set purpose. At least until you get your ducks in a row. For example, you only meet your friends from the group the second Tuesday of every month for a night of trivia. Or you get together once a month for a book club. Having another focus—one that takes the focus away from the community interaction—can allow you to build up new interest with old friends.

If you are leaving the group completely, it's pretty much the same options as any other break up. Meet face-to-face with the members of the group that you want to share this information with. Write down a list of pros and cons of being in the group prior to this meeting, so you can follow it and get your point across. Thank them for the good times. Even if you aren't going to let go of the bad times, if things don't need to be called out, then there's no need to rock the boat. After all, you are leaving. But if there are things that you feel the community could address, here's your moment to shine.

If the face-to-face doesn't work for you, a letter or phone call is always an option. Call the person who is the group president, or send an email to them, or send it to the group email list. Let them know what you loved about the group and also why you are leaving it. If you feel like you are open to contact from the group (especially if this is a group formed on a common interest), leave them your email address as a way to be in touch.

As I've said in all the other chapters, disappearing isn't cool, especially not in a community that you joined because you liked the people and possibly the mission. Even if it's an email, sending a goodbye is so much more respectful than saying nothing at all. Let everyone know that you are no longer available and around, and explain yourself. If nothing else, it won't be awkward if you run into each other again.

Real-Life Break Ups

"I helped create and shape a suspension group. We started about thirteen years ago. I was not the founder of the group, but I met the founder when I went to film a flesh hook suspension. We were young and we had this obvious connection so we began dating. That was definitely a toxic relationship.

I really admired him though. And he wanted this suspension group to be the biggest, best force to be reckoned with in the body modification world, and that's exactly what it became. I helped with all the unsexy stuff (becoming an organization, getting supplies, etc.).

After we broke up, I didn't speak to him for a year. Then his grandmother died. She was someone I cared about, and at the funeral we reconnected, this time as friends.

From there I rejoined the group and started training full on as a practitioner—as a piercer and taking blood-born pathogens, taking first aid and CPR and suturing and training with the boys. It was an 'all boys' club of ten of us, which quickly grew through the years to chapters in a number of states.

This group of people became much closer to me than my own family. When you hang from hooks you can't really talk about it with other people who haven't done it; you have to have the experience of the rush and your reasons for doing it. It's indescribable.

I always wanted the group to be more structured and

organized. I'm a fucking dominatrix. Eventually, I got put in charge of the group and everyone shut down my ideas. It was infuriating. I believe it had to do with me being a woman. I stepped down because my life was chaotic and crazy and I couldn't herd cats. Then things fell apart.

So I wrote a formal good-bye and wished everyone the best. I told them I'd still show up to events, but that I didn't want to throw events anymore. And no one really reacted to it. I'm still close with the ex-leader, because he was honest about wanting to leave, but the rest of the group I don't stay in touch with.

I learned that the community was important to them in different ways than it was to me. And while I feel like I don't have a hook family anymore, it's time to get out of my comfort zone and find my community." —Bella Vendetta

• • •

"After fifteen years, I broke up with Alcoholics Anonymous (AA). I always really loved some of the people I met and knew through AA. I had friends that really went through some hard times and had spoken honestly about the pain they experienced. At times, there was a realness there that I could relate to. There was a common bond of coming out of hell and trying to do something constructive with our lives.

When I finally realized that I was pulling away from AA, it was because I wasn't going to meetings and I didn't have a sponsor. I felt guilty about not wanting to do all of the things other AA people were doing. I just felt like it was redundant and I needed to move on, grow, and have different experiences. Also, I had a realization that I was not an alcoholic. I had definitely had bad experiences with certain hard drugs, but having been forced to identify as an alcoholic, I convinced myself that I had a drinking problem. Recently, I actually had a drink. The walls didn't cave in, I didn't die, and I didn't even throw up. It doesn't seem to be an issue for me.

I had tried one last time to work with a sponsor and that's when I knew I was done. She told me I was going to die and that my partner was a horrible person who controlled me when in reality it was my sponsor who wanted all the control. I was to go to the meetings she wanted me to go to and be at her house to "work the steps." Basically, I just removed myself from AA and most of the people I knew in AA. A lot of the people I knew had stopped talking to me anyway when they realized that I wasn't living the sober life they felt they wanted me to live.

Now, I'm actually taking better care of myself by practicing yoga, communing with nature, meditating, and being mindful. I learned that I am definitely not a joiner. I really enjoy the freedom to have the thoughts and actions I want to have. I learned that no matter what, I actually have the intuitiveness to take care of myself. It's funny how I feel more connected to people now that I'm not focusing on "my alcoholism." I feel more aware of the world and how I would like contribute to humankind in any way I can." —Angel

Taking Care of Yourself During the Break Up

Going from being part of a group that may have meant the world to you, or may have literally been your world, to being alone with your thoughts and feelings can be a really tough transition. When it comes to breaking up with community, it's super-duper important to balance staying busy with time for reflection.

Keeping a journal and then reflecting back is a great way to transition to the next place. Heck, if you started your journal before the break up, that's even better, because then you can reread the thoughts and ideas that allowed you to come to the place you're at now.

You need to show yourself ample amounts of love and respect, so do things that feel good to you. Go to the gym to get into your body. Go out dancing. Find a good yoga class or stretch routine to help you get in touch with yourself. Try making a personal altar, so you can have a visual idea of what makes you a powerful, wonderful community of one. Or build a dream board, giving yourself something to focus on in the future.

Reach out to old friends, whether they are ex-members of the same community you left or not. Go to the movies to take your mind off your own story. Plan a trip to someplace new, or a place that allows you to reconnect with your roots. And remember, you can build your own community if there isn't one that suits you. When I wanted a community of strong women around me, I invited a select group of them to become part of my Goddess Group. We got together once a month, with the intention of female bonding and empowerment. When the group became too social and gossipy, we disassembled and got together more one on one.

Still, I think of these women whenever I need support. And even after the group dispersed, it helped to remember the energy I got from them. Whatever you do to get away from your ex-community, there's a whole world out there beyond the one you knew that can bring you hope, inspiration, and comfort. Because community is everywhere, even right outside your front door.

CONSIDERATIONS FOR THE BROKEN UP

1. It's okay for people to disagree with your views. We all believe something that someone else doesn't, so deal with your feelings about your former community member's changing views.

2. You may want your former member back, but give them space to go their own way.

3. When you find yourself pushing too hard, reflect inward and determine why that push has gone to shove. What are you missing in your own life that makes you want to convince someone else that your way is the right way?

4. Talk to your community about your feelings, whether you are happy for the former member or hurt that they are gone.

5. If this brings up thoughts about getting out as well, reach out to ex-members and your own outer circle for the support you need to break up.

EIGHT

Breaking Up with Your Sexuality or Gender

*S*ex is a loaded term. When you first hear it, you probably think of the activity—the one that involves inserting "Tab A" into "Slot B." You may think of certain other acts too, or biological characteristics like hormones, reproductive organs, and genitalia. We are taught at an early age that men have penises and women have vulvas, and that, at puberty, different things happen to boys and girls.

The majority culture says sex is best between a cisgendered man and cisgendered woman (the term *cisgender* refers to a person whose gender identity matches the sex they were assigned at birth), and these two people should be in a committed relationship, preferably marriage. But looking at sex in a binary way is too limiting for some people, and it ignores a large percentage of the population who are engaging in less vanilla sex acts with people of the same, different, or varying genders. It also leaves out people who like to have sex alone (masturbation), or they don't like to have sex at all.

Understanding Sexual Orientation

Sexual orientation is how you see yourself in terms of who and what you are attracted to physically, emotionally, and romantically. It falls under the umbrella term *sexual identity*, whose other components are biological gender, gender identity, and gender role.[1] Depending on your sexual orientation, you may explore relationships with a person of the same sex, opposite sex, or with a person who identifies on a sexual spectrum. You can also have no sexual attraction to anyone at all, an identity known as asexual.

Whether you see yourself as gay, straight, pansexual, bi-curious, queer, asexual, or anything in between—your sexual orientation can shift, and if it does, your perception of yourself may shift with it.

It can feel liberating, or isolating, to break up with a sexual identity. On the one hand, you are being true to yourself and following your heart. You are giving yourself the gift of making a decision based on what feels right to you. On the other hand, you may have held on to a strong identity for a while. You may really be attached to the privilege or pride that comes with your orientation. Letting go of who you thought you were can be challenging, but embracing who you are is what life is about.

This entails taking a really deep look at how your orientation and identity impact your life. It may influence where you go to unwind based on the energy you want to be around. That doesn't mean that gay people and straight people don't mix—they do—but there is a chance you will spend more time hanging out in a place with the kinds of people who you prefer to see naked.

A change in sexual orientation can also affect how you treat yourself. You may get down on yourself for not living up to your family's, or society's, expectations of who you should be. Or you may be loving to yourself for taking care of your needs. People you know and love may also treat you differently. You need to be prepared to navigate your feelings and the feelings of those closest to you.

Understanding Gender Identity

Gender refers to the social and cultural distinctions between the sexes.

These include the roles we assign to the masculine and feminine, as well as the activities, actions, and attributes that play into these roles. Whether or not we consciously understand it, we feed into gender stereotypes all the time. For example, men are supposed to be big, strong providers, and women are supposed to be caregivers, lovers, and supporters. Now, think of athletes and nurses. What about the colors pink and blue? Are there certain gendered associations that are brought up for you?

Gender identity is our own internal sense of who we are. That can be a man, woman, a combination of the two, or none of the above. Some of us even identify with animals, including wolves, tigers, cats, and dogs. While this can sometimes be a form of sex play, there are also people who consider this an inherent part of who they are.

When it comes to gender identity, how we express ourselves externally—masculine, feminine, or other beastly—is called *gender expression*. It's generally based on the name a person uses, the pronouns they answer to (he, she, they, ze, them), and their clothing, hair, voice, behavior, and mannerisms.

A lot of people who transition from one gender identity to another know from an early age that they do not feel on the inside what they look like on the outside. Today, boys and girls as young as two and three are telling their parents, in no uncertain terms, that they are "not a boy" or "not a girl." While not necessarily a trans kid, Shiloh Jolie-Pitt's preference to be called John and be referred to as "he" is an example of a young kid breaking gender barriers.

The Concept of Fluidity

Before we begin to discuss the ways we may break up with our sexuality and gender, it can help to understand the concept of sexual and gender fluidity. The basic premise is, nothing about our sexuality or gender are written in stone, and therefore there is always the possibility that these things can change.

It may be that we have always been bi-curious and we happen

IS SEXUAL FLUIDITY A FEMALE THING?

University of Utah Psychology professor Lisa Diamond, in her 2008 book, *Sexual Fluidity: Understanding Women's Love and Desire*, explored this question in detail. She followed around a group of seventy women who identified as lesbian, bisexual, and "unlabeled" for ten years to see who they loved and made love with. She found more women joined the bisexual or "unlabeled" groups, despite the prevailing thought most would leave the terms *bisexuality* or *unlabeled* for the more concrete terms of *heterosexual* or *gay*. Her research revealed that when it came to sexual fluidity, women were more likely to go with the flow than to be stuck with a label that didn't always fit.[2]

to fall in love with someone of the same gender when we have only dated opposite-sex partners before. Or, a man, who has always had an interest in women's clothing, finally decides to slip into something more comfortable.

Fluidity can be for environmental reasons. For example, a man who only had sex with women gets sent to an all-male prison, where he now engages in sex with other men, even though he still considers himself heterosexual. It can also be that you fall for a different type of guy than you once did.

The Kinsey Scale is an often-used example of identifying sexual fluidity. The scale, created by famed sex researcher Alfred Kinsey, shows the variation of people's sexual orientation, identity, and behavior. The numbers, ranging from zero to six, represent the spectrum of heterosexual to homosexual. A person who is exclusively heterosexual becomes a zero on the scale, and a person who is exclusively homosexual is known as a six. In his sex research, Kinsey found that most people were not exclusively at either end of the scale.

The majority of people were placed somewhere in between, from a one (mostly heterosexual with potentially homosexual thoughts) to a three (a "true" bisexual) or a five (mostly homosexual with intermittent heterosexual thoughts).[3]

What it all boils down to is human beings have changing views about many things, including gender and sexuality. We all break up with parts of ourselves that no longer feel like they belong to us. We are allowed to change everything else about ourselves, from our haircuts to our jobs; from our friends, family, and community to the town, state, or country in which we live; to how we vote, eat, and exercise, why shouldn't we be permitted to do the same with our selves?

Real-Life Break Ups

"I knew something was up as early as ten or eleven. But I didn't come out until I was in my late twenties. I identify as gender queer or non-binary transgender. It was a slow process that started with me getting piercings and tattoos. Tattoos represented me taking control of my body and doing things that were deliberate and permanent. The permanent aspects appealed to me because it was me asserting something that I couldn't easily take back.

I came out to my mom on the phone. I told her that I had something important to tell her and that I wanted to be able to talk. I asked her to let me talk for a while and then told her she could ask me any questions that she wanted afterwards. After I told her, her response was very her and very lawyerly (which she is). She said, 'As long as you're not cruel—with the exception of the times we're all cruel—and as long as you don't hurt people—with the exception of the times we all hurt people—I love you just the same.' That was amazing!

I asked her to tell my dad. At the time I couldn't tell him, but my relationship with my dad has gotten so much better since coming out. I think it has to do with the fact that since I came out, I can be more honest with him, and he can be more honest with me. For example, last year on my birthday, I decided to quit grad school and wasn't sure what I wanted to do with my life. I had this amazing conversation with my dad. He told me that he was proud of me just for the courage that I had to be myself, not for a job or for an achievement.

I hope others can learn from me, and from seeing me. I wear dresses and have a 'man's' face. I dress in bold colors. I stand out and I don't outwardly display a binary gender. For so much of my life I felt shame and fear and self-hate around this. I think that's because I didn't talk to anyone about this. Honesty and truthfulness and openness are big parts of my life now, because keeping that secret all that time, I gave power to it. You don't have to talk about it with people in your life, you can find an LBGT center or group to go to. These are safe spaces where people can talk about how they feel. And just being in a room with other people who understand what you're going through, it makes you feel that you're less alone. We all struggle. It's not easy. A lot of times people say trans people are brave for coming out, but once you come out it stops being a bravery thing and starts to be a life thing." —Wee Heavy

Coming Out and Other Sex and Gender Break Ups

When who you love or how you see yourself in terms of your gender identity or sexual identity changes, you experience a "coming out." This coming out is a break up with the part of an identity that no longer serves you. It may also mean breaking up with other people who can no longer accept you for who you are.

Breaking up with our sexuality and gender requires a lot of strength and self-care. Even though there are others who can help you on this journey, this is a journey that forces you to take the steps for yourself. The process can be slow. It can be agonizingly hard and harrowing. An internal break up with external implications forces you to dissect your values and shines a mirror on the values of others. It can leave you feeling alone and questioning why your life couldn't "just be easy." But when you get out the other side, you are likely going to feel very differently.

If you decide that even though you were born male bodied, you most definitely are not a man, you are going to have to deal with your own psychological issues and accept or disconnect from your physical parts. You also have a lot of decisions to make. You need to consider how much time and money it takes to transition, if that's what you choose to do, and factor in costs for medical appointments and surgery. You may also think about voice lessons, or lessons in how to walk in high heels, so that you can do more than "pass" in society. And you'll want to think about legally changing your name on your driver's license and birth certificate.

Not only is self-acceptance huge, but getting to the place where you look and feel like yourself is a big deal. And then there is the consideration of how other people view you. Staying in a job and transitioning can be a huge challenge. There might be a lot of fear around coming out and losing your professional or social status.[4] You have to think about your safety too—not just at work or school, but also when you're out in public. You will have to deal with coworkers, family, and friends, even accepting ones, making mistakes about your pronouns. And then there's the unwanted attention from both strangers and people you know. Will you be strong enough to handle the comments, snickers, or questions like, "What are you?"

Bathrooms are another big deal. If there is no unisex bathroom, deciding which toilet to use can create huge anxiety for anyone who is transitioning.

When you're not sure if you are one gender or the other, you don't necessarily have a clear picture of how to proceed. If you're not strong enough to live your life without the acceptance of your family and friends, you may beat yourself up about who you are.

When you are ready to announce this change to the world, you often start taking hormones to physically alter your appearance. Some trans people choose to have gender confirmation surgery. Gender confirmation surgery is a big step in a gender break up, and, while it's not done by everyone, those who do it often see it as the last step to feeling affirmed and acknowledged in their identity. That could mean having breast augmentation or top surgery, which is the removal of breasts, to make a person feel more masculine. Or it could involve having genital surgery, like vaginoplasty, where a penis is removed and shaped into a vulva, or metoidioplasty, where a penis is surgically created via the extension of the clitoris.[5] Transgender pioneers include Christine Jorgensen, Kate Bornstein, Thomas Beatie, and Buck Angel, as well as Hollywood folks like *Matrix* codirector Lana Wachowski, actress Lavenere Cox, Caitlyn Jenner, and Chaz Bono. If you want to understand more about the transitioning process, check out any of their stories, or watch Amazon.com's TV show *Transparent*, which is an excellent example of the process of transitioning.

Take comfort in knowing there are people who have paved the way for you to break up with your gender or sexuality, as well as people who are doing it along with you. You are not alone, and the freedom and power that comes from being able to be your true self is not only liberating, it's also inspiring to others.

Breaking Up with the Virgin

The idea of breaking up with your sexual virginity can make any hymen shiver. Especially because many cultures try to instill in young girls' minds that sex is a big deal, and losing one's virginity will not only change your life, but will also change the way other people look at you. Virginity is such a loaded concept that losing it seems like it's going to be the most earth-shattering event in our lives. Sometimes it is a big deal, and sometimes it's not.

"There is not, and never has been, any 'official' definition of virginity, nor is there any reliable way of knowing or diagnosing whether anyone is or isn't a virgin. It all depends on what you think is going on," says Hanne Blank, author of *Virgin, the Untouched History*. "There is no way that things automatically or necessarily have to be. There is not even any real reason to think of being sexually active with a partner for the first time as 'losing' anything, you can think of it as 'gaining' a new experience too and that's just as true."[6]

Still, the message our society sends is that women and girls are worth more to other people when they are still virgins.

Virginity is such a big deal that purity balls (which pledge no sexual activity of any kind including kissing) are held in forty-eight out of fifty states.[7] At these father/daughter balls, daughters wear white and take a pledge to remain virgins until marriage, symbolically "giving" their virginity to their fathers—a sentence that even feels creepy to write.

In some countries, not being a virgin when you get married can literally cost a woman her life. Honor killings happen for a number of reasons, even when a woman is raped. It's usually because of the belief that a non-virgin brought shame or dishonor upon her family for violating the religious and cultural principle of not having sex outside of marriage, whether or not she was forced into the "violation."

These examples emphasize the idea that getting it on with a virgin is the gold standard of sexual intercourse. If you can say you've deflowered a virgin, then you're the man. When a woman can give her partner the gift of an intact hymen (even though hymens break for all sorts of reasons before a woman loses her virginity, including bike and horseback riding or using a tampon), he has received the ultimate thank-you. It doesn't have the same impact on the guy. In fact, men who are still virgins at the time of marriage are likely to be looked down upon for not getting it on. That's the double standard of the sex stigma.

This double standard can psychologically damage any woman, especially if and when she does lose her virginity, it doesn't go as planned. And sometimes even if it goes as planned, it can be disappointing.

Some people go as far as to become born-again virgins, so they can break up with their past promiscuity. They rejoice in their new-found purity and emphasize their relationship with God.

You may have also had some big expectations around the sex you were going to have, and it didn't quite turn out the way you had hoped. You will learn and grow. Blank says, "There is no truth to the idea that your first time sets the tone for the rest of your sexual life, which seems to be a common fear. And because there is no etched-in-stone definition for what 'virginity' is, if your first experience of sexuality with another person was really crappy or abusive or violent, it is totally okay to just say 'you know what, that wasn't sex, that was violence/abuse/bullshit' and to just put that in a different category."

So how else can you relieve your anxiety about losing your virginity, even if you pledge to remain a virgin until marriage?

One: Realize that virginity is a sexist concept. It doesn't impact men and women the same way. It doesn't impact lesbians and straight girls the same way. It has too many double standards and negative implications.

Two: Realize that virginity places a value on you as a person. There are lots of ways to be judged for your values, but virginity need not be one of them. Be comfortable with your decision by reading up on your body and your sexuality.

Three: If you're still struggling, talk to other people about what is bothering you, but not the people who will make you feel worse about your decision. Talk to friends who can relate to what you've gone through. Talk to a peer counselor or sex educator if you are struggling with issues around your virginity or sexuality. Go online and find other people who had similar experiences to what you're feeling. The goal is to find ways to feel less alone.

> **"** Virginity is such an outdated and unhelpful concept. Instead, we should focus on sexual debut: the first time you experienced sexuality with another being, however it was that it went. It not only opens up the avenues for a wider variety of interactions and can include everyone equally, but it also implies you made an active decision to start doing something. Nothing is lost or broken, but it's simply the start of a series of beautiful opportunities.**"**
>
> —Dr. Timaree Schmit, Sex Educator

Dealing with a Sexuality, Gender or Virginity Break Up

Transitioning your gender can take years to complete, while a sexual identity shift can happen more quickly and without much notice. Switching your sexual orientation doesn't require surgery, hormones, or other more permanent solutions. However, gender identity may involve these things, especially when the person is feeling quite confident that they are in the wrong body. Once you can identify that you are not "this person" or you are more like "that person," you can start on the road to full discovery. This is a huge topic, one that won't be adequately covered in just one chapter of a break up book. There are plenty of books and resources focused solely on these experiences. Use them in conjunction with this material for a larger understanding of your process.

> **"** There's a wonderful book called Becoming an Ex, by Helen Rose Fuchs Ebaugh. It talks about people whose identities are stated by what they were, not who they are. Ex-nun. Former man. Ex-president. Divorcee. What it taught me was that there's a need for us to establish an identity that stands on its own.

*That helped me come up with the identity of transgender.
Transgender doesn't allow for people to assume, they don't
know what direction you're talking about. They instead see that
I play with gender. It brings the focus to an identity that's cur-
rent, instead of defining me by what I used to be at one time.
Coming up with a name for your identity is important.* **"**

—KATE BORNSTEIN, AUTHOR OF *GENDER OUTLAW: ON MEN,*
WOMEN, AND THE REST OF US.

Because this is a journey of getting to know who you are, you will
have to figure a lot out for yourself. That doesn't mean you'll do it alone,
but like any big change, it can take time for other people to adjust along
with you.

Real Life Break Ups

"For most of my life I have thought of myself as a heterosexual guy
who has a few fetishes. I never really identified with the term trans-
gendered, until recently, probably because I didn't really know what
it meant.

Breaking up with being cisgendered has meant facing a lot of
embarrassment and shame—completely internalized self-judgment
and a lack of self-acceptance. A lot of this is probably leftover religious and cultural baggage that I either swallowed on my own or
was force-fed as a child. But still, I find that my relationship between
me and me is the hardest part of this work—coming out to myself
is harder than coming out to friends. I have come out to a certain
number of close friends about what I'm up to these days, and who I

think I am. Since I started, I've been told many times by people I love and respect that they are proud of me and admire me. Telling the most hidden things about myself, the things I guess I thought would alienate me or bring condemnation, has brought me support and praise. I would be doing it all regardless of what people think, but the kindness and acceptance of friends has given me hope.

Sometimes I think I should have done a lot of this work earlier in my life, but I wasn't ready. And there's one thing about doing it at age fifty: it goes to show that you can feel alive at any age, because it's not about how old you are (you have no control over that, after all). It's about showing courage, daring to grow and change, and finally getting around to doing the work you're most afraid of, but which leads to the most potential for growth and healing." —Doug

🔒

As you begin the process of breaking up, start by making a list of things that you are. Think about how you feel, and not necessarily how you look.

Get as detailed as you can about how you see yourself. Graph, or write out, what percentage of yourself adheres to certain sexual preferences or gendered ideas. List the things that make you feel good about the way you identify. Getting a clearer picture of who you are can help you get to where you're going with more confidence.

Once you get the basics down, move on to your own gender biases. For example, "I feel like a woman because I like to wear feminine clothing, especially bright-colored clothing. I also like to wear dresses and form-fitting pants."

By writing out how you see yourself, you may find out more

about yourself than you ever imagined. This type of journaling can allow for even deeper personal exploration.

♀ 🔒 ♂

Real Life Break Ups

"Two years ago, I would have said that this aspect of me—the realization that I'm more female (maybe 99 percent female) than male—emerged from my sexual orientation self-discovery, which happened in 1990. Now, I am quite sure this break up with my gender started when I was thirteen and was in full swing when I was nineteen, but that a combination of things—college, trauma, and family—effectively cut me off from that appreciation.

Before I could break up with my former identity, I had to practice self-acceptance. I had to love myself for being me, and I had to get to a place where I could follow my own path. I learned deeply from Kate Bornstein: transness is a spectrum of experience. There is no 'one experience.' Yes, it's good and important to listen to other trans persons, but their path is not your path. Learning to make your own choices is one of the most important things you can do.

I started female hormones at age sixty-two. I think I started the transition in a non-physical sense in about 2003 or 2004. I would say that I peaked in my need to break up with my male identity in November 2013. I realized that I had to do something about who I was. First, I talked to a therapist, and that was really hard to do.

Next, I talked to my doctor, which was even harder to do, but he gave me a referral to a hormone doctor and she is amazing. Once I stepped off that dime, it felt totally right.

On January 9, 2014, at 5:04 PM, I applied my first patch of estrogen. Within about an hour, I felt differently. It was, 'Bye, bye guy. Hello doll.'

'Hormones out' was pretty easy. The 'female out' part—that was a kind of 'inching forward' into the topic. The coming out process has been *really* tough in the family constellation. I have two grown kids, an ex, an older sister, and an older brother. I told my sister in April last year, she was fine. I have not told my brother and I was *petrified* about telling my kids. I told my daughter, and she understood, and so we are now very close. I have not told my son. My huge fear is total loss of that person—talk about a break up!" —Lola

When it's time to let others in on your break up, there are so many ways you can do it. You can be clever and fun and do something surprising like bake a cake and write, "I'm bisexual," in frosting on the top.[8] You can change your name on Facebook and then explain it via social media. You can write an open letter to your friends and family or call them and let them know you have something very important to tell them.

Doing it face-to-face can give you the strength to come out over and over again. Just make sure you will not be rushed or interrupted. Be prepared to answer all types of questions and deal with all sorts of feelings that might arise for you, or for the other person. This is good practice for all the other times you will have to have this conversation in your life too.

When it comes to coming out at work, you may want to ask the boss if you can hold a meeting to let those you work directly with know firsthand. Or you can shoot out a group email, explaining any changes that you need to happen going forward. For example, if you are changing your name or your pronoun, an email would be a good place to let people know how you'd like to be addressed.

One thing is certain: you will come out again and again, so learn to do it with confidence. After you take some time with yourself, tell your close friends about your decision. In fact, make the first person you tell the person you can feel safest with. And remember, it gets better.

Expect Some Rejection

While you will have a lot to say on the subject of your sexuality, let others explore how they feel as well. Ask them what it means to them to hear you say that you are straight, gay, bi, pansexual, queer, etc. If it's no big deal to them, there's no need to make it a big deal for your relationship with them either. Devote as much time as necessary to process your decision with those closest to you. Some people may be completely overwhelmed by the information, so be prepared to give some of your friends and family space to come to acceptance. And while hopefully they will, there is a chance that they won't. Or you may decide that even though they accept you, your relationship with them was based on certain gender assumptions (i.e. a beer club is for *guys* who drink beer), and you may no longer want to associate with them. And although there could be a sense of rejection from some, you can find a community that embraces your "you" as you are.

Real-Life Break Ups

"I thought I was a full-blown lesbian until I was twenty-one. I was completely immersed in the Maryland lesbian community for years— and then when I started suspecting that I could be attracted to guys,

I tried men out, and found that they're not as icky as I originally thought. I hid my bisexuality from the community for a while because I was afraid of their reaction. Bisexual women are often thought to be 'loose' and indecisive because they 'can't choose' between men and women. Lesbians are particularly threatened by bisexuals because they think bi women are often just 'experimenting' with lesbianism. Getting into a relationship with a bisexual woman is considered risky, because there's a chance she may leave her lesbian girlfriend for a guy.

When I finally did come out as bisexual, the lesbian community shunned me. My confession was met with sneers and disappointed expressions. A common reaction was, 'Oh no! We lost another one,' like I was a casualty of sexual war.

When I told my straight male friends about my bisexuality, some of them were like, 'Oh yeah! Now I have a chance to do it with you!' while others were wigged out and acted like they didn't know who I really was; they felt like I'd lied to them. One dude had a crush on me for a while and was upset that I didn't ask him out as soon as I realized I liked dudes. He held it against me and we haven't spoken for years.

In a way, being a part of the lesbian community was like being a part of a strict religion. I could say and do whatever I wanted, as long as I accepted vagina as my sexual savior.

When I discovered I was bisexual, I had to break up with my lesbian community—and make it a clean break. The community only wanted me to hang with them if I could commit to being gay forever.

And I just couldn't give my life to the Chapel of Cha-Cha. Needless to say, I don't talk to anybody from the lesbian scene anymore. It's a shame, but the community was judgmental and limiting. That relationship had to end." —Krissy

🔒

Some people may break up with you for changing. You'll have to accept this too, and deal with it as someone who is being broken up with. It can and does happen, and just as you're asking them to accept you, you have to respect their decision to be unaccepting.

Come up with a back up plan in case the rejection becomes too much to handle. Have the name of a support person, someone you know well or a professional. If it's a friend, make sure they know when you're planning on having a difficult conversation, so they can be standing by when it's all done.

It's always good to talk to a professional too. It can help you stay clear and move forward with your process. Attending a support group can also be very empowering.

Ultimately, you need to make the choices that work best for you, and if whom you love and whom you screw screws with how others see you, then that's their own issue to deal with. Respect others for having their opinions, but always respect yourself most.

CONSIDERATIONS FOR THE BROKEN UP

1. It's okay to ask for clarity around concepts, as long as you are non-judgmental and open to learning.
2. Give yourself permission to ask questions or have feelings.
3. This is a chance for you to explore your own assumptions around sex and gender too.
4. It's not okay to try to convince somebody that their feelings aren't valid.
5. Seek out experienced help to deal with your feelings on the subject too.

NINE

Breaking Up With Your Career

We spend a majority of our lives working. Sometimes we're working on ourselves or working toward a goal whether it be to find a cure for a disease, to make money to live a comfortable life, to lose weight or learn to stop using the word *should*. But for the majority of us, working means getting paid to do a job for someone else or for ourselves in order to make a living. A majority of people building a career are success-driven, meaning we are working toward a goal.

We spend a lot of our time defining ourselves by what we do "for a living." This is a very American thing (or so I've been told). It's often one of the first questions we find ourselves asking, or being asked, in conversation with someone we don't know all that well. The fact that we focus so much attention on "what we do," and not on who we are, makes breaking up with a job or a career a pretty big deal.

The workplace can offer us a lot of opportunities. It provides us with a place to function as an individual or on a team. It affords us the opportunity to develop a set of skills, or find out more about something that interests us. It's a space where we can feed off the energy of others who share a common goal. It's a place where we are given responsibilities that we don't usually have at home, as well as a place we can go to get away from home. The workplace is a chance for us to identify as something beyond our family and our friends, and it's a place where we can try on and take off various hats. Some people find one job and stick with it throughout their lifetime, but others of us use work to experience, learn, and move on when the time is right.

Either way, when our working relationships stop working, they are broken. And if you can't see fixing the relationship, it may be time for a break up. Sometimes a break up isn't your choice—you may get fired or let go for reasons beyond your control. But other times you may become disillusioned with your job, need a new adventure, or just want a change.

Real-Life Break Ups

"It's incredibly difficult to try to make acting into a career. You can work extremely hard at it and not get anywhere, even if you're unbelievably talented, which I'm not. I'm a good actor but not a great one. I got really tired of not being in the unions, not having representation, not landing any gigs that were moving me forward, going to open calls where I'd wait for two hours to be seen for two minutes, and doing work that I was embarrassed to tell anyone I was in. The proverbial straw that broke this actor's back was when I shot a reality television pilot, thinking it would be fun and that I'd be seen by millions of people on TV. Instead, the entire shoot was a complete nightmare and the show never aired. I came home and I was done.

Breaking up was easy and hard. I cancelled my subscription to *Backstage*, got off all the acting mailing lists I was on, stopped sending headshots and resumes, and recycled most of what I had left. Turning off my voicemail was harder and getting rid of my acting website was *really* hard.

The worst part was dealing with the realization that my dream was gone; the thing that I had been trying to do and be for years and years no longer was a part of my life. I felt completely empty. I had (and still have) no idea what else I'd want to do, besides nothing. When I got to actually act and be paid for it, it wasn't like a job, it was just how life was supposed to be. I was really depressed (much worse than normal) for around two months. I probably should have gone into therapy.

I don't miss the grind at all. I only miss having a purpose, as I still don't feel like I really have one. Being a father helps, but it's not quite it." —Josh

The Difference Between a Job and a Career

A job is usually an employment situation where there is limited, if any, room for personal growth. It usually doesn't require special training or education, or if it does, you can generally learn these things while "on the job."

A career can be made up of a series of jobs, but it's also a path to achieving goals on a road you're passionate about taking. It's generally a long-term concept that requires additional training and is salaried. A job is usually based on hourly pay.

You can go from job to job and feel like a cog in the machine, but if you jump from job to job with a focus on your career, you will feel more like you are a necessary component in how the machine functions.

A bad job might mean you look for something else of equivalent pay, while a bad career can contribute to a ton of stress, anxiety, and depression. Still, if you stick with a job or career that doesn't suit you, both may lead to feelings of regret and remorse when it comes to life satisfaction.

Changing Careers: An All-Ages Decision

We experience a lot of stress over career changes, mostly because we need money to live or because we have become disinterested in something we were once passionate about. As we get older, we usually have more responsibility, and this responsibility tends to hold us back from making big, life-changing decisions. While responsibility requires sacrifice, it also requires we achieve a level of satisfaction so we can stay productive. And even if this responsibility makes breaking up with a career seem like something only younger folks can afford to do, it's important that people of any age be happy with their career choices.

I have broken up with more careers that most of my friends. I started out with the dream of being an on-air radio personality (a career I pursued right out of college) before moving on to becoming a radio and TV producer, and then a well-known sex educator. I also pursued graduate school to become a sex and relationship therapist, finishing up my PhD in sex education at the same time. Each step has led me to set new goals and pursue another part of myself.

Of course, at the time of all of my big decisions, I was single and only had myself to care for. Now, as a mother, that isn't the case. Still, I'd do it again, with the caveat of making sure I saved up some money to be able to have a level of cushioning. The question is, would you?

It can be inspiring to watch yourself pursue a new career and head further down your path. Once you commit to heading down your new road, you will have a sense of pride in being true to yourself. It may be hard to imagine taking big career risks in your forties and fifties, but it's not unfathomable. Sure, it may look like a mid life crisis, but it could also be a mid life catharsis.

What to Know Before You Go

It's not always possible to break up with a career, or even a job. Especially when you have a family to support, bills to pay, and no clear picture regarding how you can save money in the present while working toward your future. In fact, it would be pretty scary to start anew when you don't have the support you need to get by. Sometimes, the best way to start going through the process is to seriously think about what it is you want to do and make a timeline of achievable steps toward your goal.

Unless you're single and/or working for yourself, a career change will impact your family, your roommates (when they ask how you'll pay the rent), and even your coworkers. If you're partnered, you need to be willing and able to talk with your partner so they can help figure out your financial situation for the time being. And you want to make sure you're doing what feels right to you.

♦ 🔒 ♦

Real-Life Break Ups

"I came to the conclusion that I was in the wrong career one morning at about 2 AM. I was still awake at my computer doing some freelance web development work and loving it. I thought back to earlier in the day, staring at the clock, unsatisfied writing copy and proofreading ads. I decided then that work could be fun, and that I didn't need to be stuck in my dead-end job. So, I started educating myself through online courses and Meetup groups.

It was so important to develop my network. I had to go out and meet people in the industry and learn new skills. It was not easy, and it's even harder as you get older and have more responsibilities. I made the change when I was thirty, married, and a homeowner. But I wanted it bad enough, so I found the time and made the sacrifices. I found out how little sleep I could function on. I used vacation days to work on projects, attend conferences, and go to networking events. I did this until I was confident enough to make the break from copywriting to becoming a professional web developer.

The hardest part was the unknown. I was scared. I'd only had one professional job after graduating from college and I was there for a long time, and now I was leaving for a new career with a new skill set in New York City. As a copywriter, I worked in an industrial park in the suburbs of New Jersey, so working in NYC was big and scary in and of itself. I drove to work in NJ; now I was going to take a bus. I had no idea how the subway worked. I was also married and owned a condo, so there was that stress too if things didn't pan out. However, I had a wife who pushed me and supported me. She pushed me to leave my job since she knew I hated it. She worked in NYC prior to becoming a freelancer, so she told me where things were in the city and how to get around. The fact that she was onboard and supporting this decision made it easier to deal with the transition.

All this investment paid off. Now, I rarely feel like my job is 'work,' since even if I had millions of dollars and didn't have to work anymore, I'd still be at my computer writing code for something. I almost feel like my previous career was some sort of bad dream. And

even if I'm having a tough day in my new career, I'd take it over the

best day at my previous career." —Michael

The more certain you feel about your decisions, and the more support you have, the better able you will be to handle any challenges that arise, including the challenge of making the wrong decision and finding out that you didn't really want to go anywhere. To stop doubt from creeping in, there are some preventative measures you can put into place. These can help you make sure that you don't quit your current job until you're ready to start anew.

TALK TO YOUR FAMILY

Your family's support will be integral during this time of change. And since they will be impacted by your decision, talk with them before making any drastic moves. Even if you are miserable and really need a change, you need to lay out a plan of action for how you will pay rent, bills, and other expenses that you usually cover.

TALK WITH A PROFESSIONAL

A life coach is great at helping you flush out what you think is your purpose and then can help you find ways to succeed. A career consultant can help you map out a plan for exploring new options and keep you moving forward on your path.

USE HUMAN RESOURCES

If you want to stay in the same organization but might want to be handling different responsibilities, talking with someone in Human Resources could help facilitate the shift you need.

TAKE A LEAVE OF ABSENCE

Find out what your company's policies are for paid or unpaid leave. During that time, you can research other job options or decide about going back to school. Time away from work not only allows you to see what's realistic and viable; it also gives you a chance to make sure you don't act too hastily.

VOLUNTEER

Spend a few hours once a week donating your services to someplace or something that lifts you up. Or, if you have the money or flexibility, leave your job and volunteer someplace tropical or exotic. You never know when you may be able to volunteer your way to a new career path. By creating a working vacation, you can volunteer your time and services in a place you've always wanted to visit and try out a job you never thought possible.

WRITE IT OUT

If you're uncertain about why you're leaving or what to do next, write it down. First, write a list of the reasons you should stay and the reasons you want to go. Then, write down careers you'd really like to have. It's not important that you know specifics. For example, you don't need to know that you want to help people work out their tax problems; just knowing you want to help people is a good start. You can also get ideas from things you do in your free time. Staying home and watching movies could be an indication that a job that doesn't require a lot of travel is right up your alley.

DO YOUR RESEARCH

Peruse LinkedIn and other social networking sites to follow the careers of people you admire, and look into other job sites to get an even better idea of what's available. Talk to people in your proposed future career, and let them know that you are interested in changing fields. Offer to buy them coffee or a meal so you can probe them for any advice, suggestions, and job leads. Find out what kind of trainings and conferences you can attend that will help you enhance your skills and connections. Join listservs or Meetup groups that share your interests. You might also want to check into costs associated with these expenditures and any credentials you will need for success down the road.

CREATE A KICK-ASS CV
Write a resume that shines light on the strengths you have. Are you a master at working on a team? Or are you a well-known problem solver? Highlight your leadership and people skills to get you where you want to go. Seek inspiration in what you love doing, and you can find a career in doing what you love.

FIND YOUR HAPPY PLACE
Be at peace with the fact that you are likely starting back at the beginning. And even though you are going to be starting from the ground and working your way back up, don't let age, or other people, stop you from enjoying the experience of learning new skills. When it comes to careers, it's better to be climbing up a ladder than sliding down a chute.

Breaking Up with the Workplace
When it's time to leave your job or career, stand strong and remain calm. Keep your game face on, and if you're wavering, remember why you're leaving (go back to your list of pros and cons if you've written them down). Discuss any doubts you have with your support network. Take a deep breath, and think of all the things that led up to this decision. Then leave the job knowing that you are in the driver's seat on this one.

While you may never care to return, it's better to break up on good terms than bad ones. If you know you're going to break up with your job, get as much work done as you can (or care to) so you can ensure there is a letter of recommendation waiting for you whenever you need it. And, just in case you might want to come back, breaking up on good terms is more likely to allow you the opportunity to knock on an open door in an emergency.

♦ 🔒 ♦

Real-Life Break Ups

"In October 2013 there was an opening within our marketing department for a digital marketing director. I expressed interest in the position but because the position was never posted, I could not formally apply.

At the same time I was broadening my search and opening up possibilities of where I wanted to work. My wife actually found a YMCA position and I applied. To my amazement I got a response and started the interview process.

Move ahead to the middle of November and I was now a final candidate for the YMCA job. One Monday night at work, I was on our internal employee site looking for someone's title within the organization (I was working at a large TV network). I was clicking around and noticed that the position that I had expressed interest in had been filled. The next morning I confronted my boss on the matter. To my knowledge there were no interviews for this position. He did not have an answer.

At the same time the Y had started doing reference checks. Finally, on Friday morning I got an answer from the GM of the television network that yes, they had filled the position. I expressed my displeasure in how the situation was handled and that I was not upset that someone else had filled the job, but how I was never given a shot to interview for it. That afternoon I received the offer from the YMCA. I called my wife and told her.

I accepted the position that Friday. That following Monday I went into my boss's office with my letter of resignation then went down to the GM's office and informed him of my decision to leave. I put in the two weeks notice and haven't looked back.

The hardest part was leaving coworkers that I had worked with for long periods of time, as well as leaving the comfort zone of the TV/entertainment world to go market the YMCA. Change is hard, it took me three years to finally leave. I would recommend to anybody to network, reach out to past coworkers, and leave on good terms." —Gavan

🔒

If you think some of your coworkers are going to take the news personally, try to tell them before word spreads like wildfire. Before you go into your boss's office, have an email pre-typed and ready to send out immediately after your meeting. If you have made close friends at work, you can use the email to set up a time and date for a good-bye gathering at a local bar or restaurant. You can also create a monthly get-together so you have some assurance you will stay in touch after you leave and you won't miss out on the office gossip and other adventures. When it comes to discussing your decision to leave with your coworkers, be honest about your reasons for leaving without bashing the company (even if the company deserves a good bashing). Not everyone will have the same opportunities as you, and although some of your coworkers may want out as well, they may not have the strength or drive to make it happen. And if they like where they work, they may not feel comfortable hearing you talk trash about their employer. While your coworkers may be sad to see you go, they will hopefully be excited that you are moving on your path.

When it comes to actually leaving a job, the only real choice is to break up face-to-face, unless you work remotely. If that's the case, you can let them know by phone or over email. Regardless, be courteous. Even if you absolutely detest the tasks you had been assigned and can't wait to rip off your uniform and burn it in a ritual beach bonfire with your friends (remember burning clothes can be bad for the environment), stay gracious and grateful during your exit interview. When quitting, thank those above you for investing their time and energy in your work. If you can, point out an example or two of good impressions they have left on you. And then, if you need to, you can always express your discontent in the nicest way possible.

If they hire someone new after you leave, think about if you would be open to getting a call from your replacement, so that you can show them the ropes. Look at the situation, and ask yourself how you would want others to act if they were the ones leaving you at the job.

Unfortunately, we don't always leave jobs for personal gain, but even when you're leaving for more difficult reasons—like having to take care of a sick parent or child—people are generally open to helping make the transition smoother both for you and for them. And while not all break ups are about bad bosses or office policies, some of them are. If your break up is about how your boss mistreats you, or because of your company's policy on covering birth control for women, you may not leave quietly and nicely. And that's okay too. But, as the saying goes, you get more flies with honey than with vinegar.

Breaking Up with a Business Partner

When you cocreate a concept or business with another person, it's like being married and making a baby. And although you don't walk down the aisle thinking about who would get the child if you decide

ARE YOU SATISFIED?

When it comes to job satisfaction, singing makes people happy. According to a study on myplan.com,[1] singers report the highest levels of gratification from their work. Fire fighters are the second most satisfied, followed by aircraft assemblers (Who knew?), pediatricians, college professors, and counselors. The most unhappy in their jobs are clerks of many kinds (including mail clerks, municipal clerks, insurance policy processing clerks, and hotel desk clerks). Housekeepers and those who work in the food service industry were also low down on the satisfaction scale.

to divorce (or if you do, you might want to reconsider the marriage), when it comes to a business relationship, it usually works better to figure those details out before you jump into the union. As a result of the strong bond of business, a break up with a business partner can drain you of a whole lot of emotion and money. Having safeguards in place beforehand can help with the heartache.

Just like in marriage, signing some sort of business "prenup" is a good plan. Otherwise, you may not realize just how entangled you are and how complicated the mess is that you need to get out of. Money and pride can cloud your judgment about right and wrong. Whether the break up is due to health or hate, there are going to be things that need to be addressed fairly. That's why you might want to really consider working with a mediator, attorney, accountant, or advisor.

If you can stay levelheaded through the break up, you can address your concerns, fears, and feelings. If one partner did things that seemed unethical, it's important to address this too, and a third person can help hold a safe space for you. That may mean you need to bring up things your partner may have been doing, including making deals on the side or hiding finances from you. Or maybe you just want to take the business in a different direction and need to break up with a business partner so you can do that.

There are other big things you want to think about, too, like do either of you get to carry on with the business as planned? What happens to the name and the concept when you go kaput? Are you willing to be bought out, or does the idea die when the ship goes down? All of this requires planning and consent from all those involved. The best approach is an honest approach, but not one that is motivated by anger or hate. Even if there are ugly reasons to end the relationship, trying to find the solution that works in the best interest of the "baby" will allow you to see things through a bigger-picture approach.

Being Broken Up With: Getting Fired or Laid Off

When your career breaks up with you, it's just as stressful as the sudden end to a romantic relationship. You need time to grieve and to accept the situation. If your identity has been wrapped up in your company or your position, then leaving can feel like dying. But the silver lining is that you now have the chance to be reborn.

In order to go through the process of mourning the loss of who you were (based on your career), you need to feel the loss. You may need to go to the gym and punch a heavy bag or have a good cry. Perhaps you want to find a way to signify the ending of a chapter in your work life by performing a ritual tearing up of your old business cards and other mementos. Or maybe you need to recite a mantra reminding yourself that you will survive.

You'll want to stay busy too. You can join groups that promote your passions, whether they are related to the job you just lost or the job you want to find. You may also want to practice how you handle the "identity dilemma" when it comes up in conversation. Think about what you will say when someone asks, "What do you do?" What other things do you love to do? What are your hobbies? And what are you hoping to do now that you have the freedom to find a new path?

If you've been fired or laid off, you may not have much time to get out (both your stuff and your person). This can happen when you quit too, especially when the company sees your staying as a threat to their "top-secret" business. Either way, try to get away from work before you laugh out loud or lose your shit. And before you do anything drastic, sit with the news. You may feel hurt, angry, lost, rejected, unworthy, or undesirable. On the flip side, you may feel elated, free, excited, and motivated to move on. Whatever it is you're feeling, really feel it.

Make sure you take everything important with you. Get clear on what type of severance pay is owed to you and what else you deserve when you leave. Also, ask for a letter of recommendation if you can.

Once you get out of there, get *out*. This could mean going to a park or a movie or locking yourself in a closet to cry and contemplate your next move. Basically you want to go someplace where you can be alone with your feelings and thoughts so that you can have some time to think things through. If that idea seems too depressing, go someplace where you can be mentally but not physically alone. That may mean going to a yoga class to get your zen on or to a bar to have a drink, as long as you try not to drink yourself into a stupor (even if it feels like the best thing you can do).

Heading home and straight to bed is also an option, or going down to the basement and making your own (wo)man cave works too. But you can't stay there for days on end, because it won't help you get out of the funk. If you don't live alone, explain to your family or roommates that you need a little alone time and that you'll come around when you're ready. If they insist on knowing what's going on, firmly set your own boundaries while also letting them know that you will be okay. Then give them a hug and head off and be proud that you practiced being the boss of you.

Share the news when you can with the assurance that you will be okay. And if you need assurance from someone else, phone or text someone who has always been a fan of yours, not someone who has put you down and will "tell you so" again.

As you get more comfortable with the idea of change, you'll be able to hear advice, get support, or even find a lead on a new job from those closest to you and their connections. After you feel confident everything will be all right, or at least that you can hold it together for the time being, let anyone that was impacted by your work know that you are no longer at the same job. This can mean telling everyone from your coworkers (who may already know), to the contacts you made through work, to the competitors, and even your local barista. You never know where your next job lead will come from.

Real-Life Break Ups

"For nearly two decades before becoming a sexuality educator, I was with one of the world's top advertising agencies. During my last few years at the agency I attended quite a few good-bye parties for coworkers who left their lucrative careers for something more fulfilling. Some opened bakeries, travel businesses, or simply began freelance consulting from home. I was at burnout levels too and envied those who found a way to put their happiness first. Ultimately, I remained at my job because I lacked the courage to follow in my brave coworkers footsteps. I kept telling myself being a single working mom with a mortgage, I had too much responsibility to quit my job for a carefree life with no guaranteed security. All that changed with a layoff.

Being unexpectedly unemployed was terrifying. It was also the best thing that could have ever happened to me, although it didn't feel like it at first. I decided right then and there this was my only chance to make a change. It was now or never. It was quite a process redefining my identity. I spent all of my time devouring information—self studying human sexuality and learning how to market myself in this new arena. I was forced to figure out who I was, once I was stripped of my 'corporate mom' label. The transition was a slow process. Every day I wondered if I made the right decision not to go back to agency life. Every day, however, it got a bit easier and I grew more confident.

Fast-forward seven years. I am not only the happiest I've ever been but happier than I thought possible. And my happiness keeps growing exponentially. I didn't realize how much my previous career was sucking the life out of me until that career was long gone. The majority of my work I do from home at my own pace. I have more time for my family. I laugh and smile more and feel absolutely free. I still do work a lot, but work doesn't feel like work. As a result, I get more done allowing me to achieve an incredible amount of success in a short amount of time. Leaving my previous career behind was the best decision I've ever made and it's enhanced mine and my children's lives tenfold. If I knew then what I know now, I would have left my job years before that lucky layoff." —Sunny Megatron, sex educator and TV personality.

● ● ●

"It wasn't my choice. I got dumped. I got laid off along with half the staff (the other half were laid off the following year). It was the push that I needed but I wasn't in any way ready for.

The hardest part was that I had no say in the matter. I had a one-year-old son and owned a home, and it was terrifying to have to figure out my next move. I sent resume after resume with very little interest. The fact was I didn't really want any of those jobs; I wanted the one I had.

My husband was helpful in dealing with the mechanics of it all—the resumes, juggling schedules for interviews, etc. But (as much as I love him) he lacks a bit of empathy sometimes, and I felt like I was on my own emotionally. Most of my friends were in the industry. If they were employed it was hard for me to turn to them. Many of them were also unemployed at the same time, and it was too depressing to all be together. I was trapped in a funk for a while.

It was like breaking up a relationship, but usually after a relationship you can take all the time you need before dating again. You can dabble a bit in the dating scene and have conversations or hook-ups without committing or making any decisions. Here I had no choice but to jump back into the game. I eventually landed a gig in a related field that paid excellent money, but on day one, I knew I had made a big mistake. Three months in I was still miserable—the people, the environment, the work—none of it was what I was used to or what I wanted. I came from a job where every day was fun, or had some form of excitement, and this job was not how I wanted to spend more than one-third of my time.

I had been considering going back to school but was having

a hard time dropping it all to start from scratch. My husband's new job salary and moving to a cheaper city afforded us the opportunity for me to take the time, grow our family some more, and go to school.

It's been three years now. Other than missing family and old friends, I am happier than ever—with new friends and a lovely (though sometimes boring) place to raise children. I miss the old job. But I think of it like a starter marriage: it served its purpose at the time, but it wasn't ever going to be sustainable for the long-term life I wanted. I don't want to work those hours anymore. I don't want corporate drama. I don't want to spend my life making rich people richer. So this time around my plan is to spend my days making people's lives better, and being home at the end of the day with my family." —Naomi

🔒

Change can be exciting. And yeah, it can also scare the pants off of you. But because you have no choice in this matter, getting the scary part out of the way will help you evaluate the exciting bits to come. Being fired can mean you weren't particularly passionate about the position you were in. If that's the case, this is a chance to find something you like more. And if being fired was about clashing with your boss, then you don't have to deal with him or her again.

If you were let go because of major layoffs or the company went under, and your job isn't so specific that there is only one or two positions like yours in the entire state, hopefully you can find a similar job. And if you can't, then maybe this is the opportunity you needed to create your own job and work for yourself. You can reinvent yourself by going back to school or, as you look for work, volunteer some place you always wanted to know more about (like an animal shelter or community garden). You can update your CV and get right back up and on the workhorse. Or you can decide on the next career you want and find a way to make it happen.

Moving On

In any instance, a strong support network is integral. Having partners, friends, and family who can help support you on your journey is essential for getting by. If you don't already have a list of people you can count on, write one now. You don't need to include more than three to five people, but having an emergency backup list for any situation can help you feel less alone. While it can be hard to ask for help, we all get by with help from others. And however you break up with a career or a job, connection is key.

Real-Life Break Ups

"I couldn't believe that I was thinking about breaking up with my job as a columnist at a major magazine. I was passionate about my topic and had become respected as one of the experts in the field—I even wrote two books and had a regular spot on a radio show for a while. After all the work I'd done to achieve my goal, I was going to quit?

But I was, and I did.

What shocked me was how deeply I felt the loss of my identity, and how long it took me to stop defining myself as 'I used to be a columnist . . .' And then one day at a party, about three years later, the inevitable question came: 'What do you do?' and I said,

'Technical writing and horses.' And it wasn't until a friend burst out

laughing and said, 'And also she's written two books and had a

magazine column,' that I realized I had totally forgotten to define

myself by my past." —Regina

🔒

And even if your job was your identity, having to create a new persona could be exciting and fulfilling.

You may find you're less afraid to take risks, especially since you have already lost a lot. This resilience can lead you to pursue your path with gusto. And remember, lots of successful second and third careers have happened as a result of getting kicked in the ass—and out the door—at work.

According to a recent job satisfaction survey, less than 50 percent of workers are satisfied with their jobs.[2] Ultimately, if you can find satisfaction in a job well done, then you're winning at work.

CONSIDERATIONS FOR THE BROKEN UP

1. While a job may give you a certain identity, leaving a job allows for the space to create a new identity.
2. Be gracious when leaving. Don't badmouth bosses and coworkers, even if they deserve it.
3. Seek out support. Let people know what you're doing, or looking to do, next.
4. Be prepared to get all sorts of emotional about the ending of an era (whether at the company you work for or in the career you once had).
5. Remember that reinvention is reinvigorating.

TEN

Breaking Up with Anyone Else

Once you've broken up with the things you've been committed to for at least a portion of your life (whether it be your career, your cousin, or your community), breaking up with anyone else may seem easy breezy.

Either way, the little people in your life—meaning those who occupy only a certain amount of your space and time—are still people in your life. They are the people in your neighborhood, the barista who makes you coffee every morning, or the person you see every six weeks to wax your pubic hair. If you have a relationship with someone and then you don't want them to rip the hair out of your skin any longer, it doesn't mean they don't deserve some sort of fond farewell.

The reality is, we're not going to get all "official" when it comes to ending a relationship with our psychic (who should be able to predict it anyway, right?) or our bank teller (check). And if we visited a dentist two times and our teeth decided they needed some fresh fluoride, is there really a reason to tell the dentist that we're not coming back for another cleaning? Probably not. But sometimes we establish a relationship with someone that goes a bit beyond casual acquaintance.

You may not call your favorite fitness trainer every weekend to let her know if you're feeling sore from this week's workout. But if you regularly attend a class or try personal training a couple of times and establish a relationship with this person, it may be awkward when you see them at the gym, or they see you stuffing your face with a doughnut, a month after you last got physical.

Maybe you can handle the occasional run-in with a hairdresser you cut out of your life. If you can sweep the ugly under the rug every time you run into your former housekeeper, then sweep away. But it's better not to have to worry about what happens when you two do see each other. It's easier when you don't have to pretend you care or don't care. Just lay it on the line, and you will know what line you walk on.

Breaking up with these people is a matter of how far you're willing to go to give them the courtesy of letting them go. Nobody's perfect in this arena (or in any area of breaking up, really). But, if the person you are about to break up with ever just pops up in your thoughts, then they probably wouldn't mind being told you're moving on. And if you've known someone long enough to feel like they are a part of your life, or at least a part of your routine, do you just change up the schedule without letting them know there's been a change of plans?

This Sounds Ludicrous, Right?

Okay, breaking up with anyone else may seem like a stretch, especially because it's easier to just let things slide without making a big deal about endings and beginnings. It's already challenging to break up with those people you really care about, so why break up with the people you care less about?

While you may not sweat the small stuff, it is little things in life that sometimes matter. Most of these break ups don't require a long, drawn-out understanding of what transpired. Breaking up with anyone else may just be a great way to have closure and move on. Smaller break ups are a significant way to move forward and can prove to have a larger meaning for you, in your life.

Breaking up with someone allows both of you the opportunity to grow. For the person doing the breaking up, it gives you a chance to practice being honest and open with someone, even when it's awkward or difficult. And it gives them a chance to examine their behavior too, especially if there's something they did, or didn't do, that made you decide you were done using their services. Offering feedback in a constructive (and not critical) way can allow them to grow as a provider and you to grow as a communicator.

I know that if someone I see all the time just drops out of sight, I wonder what happened and hope that they are still alive and well. Yeah, I do think about if they died, which may be a stretch in terms of places to go in my mind, but it does happen. And if I think like that, then I'm not the only one. Saying good-bye will, if nothing else, alleviate a morbid curiosity about what has happened to you. Even if you've only scheduled three sessions with your Pilates instructor, thanking them (in the end) and letting them know it's over brings closure and clarity.

Some people deserve to know because these people have helped you get ahead in your life. Whether it's by taking care of your children or your house, it's quite immature to stop using their services without letting them know why you're done—especially if they may rely on what you pay them to help get by. Sure, it's easy to make up an excuse, but telling someone that it's not them (when it is) or that you'll call them the next time you need them (when you won't) leaves them waiting on your call or hoping things change. Even if they're not desperately seeking your patronage, the fact that you couldn't just be up front with them means that there are probably other places in your life where you're avoiding things.

♀ 🔒 ♂

Real-Life Break Ups

"When my daughter was only three months old and I was returning to work, my sitter pulled out on me. I was wary of trusting her to begin with, but a working parent is so beholden to the childcare provider and even those not-so-perfect situations have to be palatable. So when I quickly found Fran to take her place, a local young mother of two, she was like a dream for me.

Fran was smart, sweet, and energetic and there was never a day when I didn't feel totally secure dropping my 'most precious' off at her home. There's a kind of security, an intimacy, that comes with a caretaker relationship that can be special when perfect, and devastating when it is somehow taken away. For eight hours a day, Fran was the mother I couldn't be. So to say that I was in a relationship with her pretty succinctly gets at the heart of it.

Fran watched my daughter from three months until just shy of her second birthday. On the day she 'broke up with me,' I received a text from her saying that she needed to talk to me that afternoon, and my heart dropped. I cried the whole way to her house, knowing the substance of what she would tell me, and not knowing where I would go from there. As it turned out, her home was going to be foreclosed on, and she and her family needed to move in with her in-laws.

I went into panic mode from there. Could I buy her house in foreclosure and simply rent it back to her? Could we advance her money to help her situation? The truth was that there was nothing I could do. She was a twenty-six-year-old mother of two with a husband working as an assistant manager in the butcher department of the local grocery store. I couldn't change her situation just to suit my own, and so I had to let her go. But as it turned out it wasn't that simple.

A month after her last date of service, I decided to reach out to her because my daughter kept asking for her and her children. Would she like to maybe just meet up at the mall in the play area? She said yes and we set a date, though not a time. So that weekend when I texted her three times and emailed her to find out what the plan was, I was surprised that I never got a response. Something had happened, and it was out of my hands. She had no presence on social media, so I couldn't even find out there. Yet I kept trying. Every few months, I Googled her just to see what came up. One day I discovered an obituary for her father-in-law, so I wrote it off as family issues. Though I never quite felt settled.

I truly felt like she had in some way abandoned me, which made absolutely no sense because she was an employee, end of story. But she cared for my child and loved her, so I think in my mind it couldn't be end of story. In some way, the sense of trust that I had put in her seemed somehow misplaced, simply knowing that she was gone and never wanted to know what became of my daughter. It was illogical. But I stopped Googling, I stopped emailing, I stopped looking for her.

And then one day we saw her.

A year after our last contact, we were in our local supermarket, and my husband spotted her from behind, along with her two children. I sprinted across two aisles just to stop her, and when she turned around it all hit me. She was thin—too thin. And she was pregnant again. She fumbled for excuses as we greeted. She mentioned that her Crohn's disease had flared up and she was in doctor's offices twice a week. The house never foreclosed and they were moving back in. She couldn't work. And she was eight months pregnant. And I suddenly realized that she hadn't dumped my daughter or me—she just had a life, and a difficult one at that. I smiled and told her, 'Sometimes it's harder to reach out to someone and give them the whole story than it is to just get through your every day. It's really good to see you and know that you are okay.' She looked relieved and smiled. I wished her luck and said good-bye." —Amy

🔒

Why Do These Relationships End?

Sometimes relationships end because we aren't satisfied with the service or the service provider. Other times it's an issue of location or relocation. When we move, we may not be able to get to our favorite massage therapist any longer.

Another reason these relationships end is because of scheduling conflicts. Whether it's a performer who you've hired for your kid's birthday party and they decide at the last minute they can't show up, or a doctor who can never fit you in at a good time for you, sometimes we don't have to break up with people for what they've done but instead for what they can't do.

In these situations, you've got a good excuse and an easier way out. And when it's not necessarily personal, by all means ask them to refer you to someone who fits your requirements. Asking them for help can show the other person that you value their opinion and suggestions. However, if you can't stand them on top of the fact that you can't get a schedule that fits both your needs, then let them go and be glad they're gone.

How to Break Up

If you're not on a first-name basis with someone, the relationship just ends and it's pretty straightforward. But if you have one-on-one experiences with this person—meaning they know where you live, how many children you have, where your dog likes to poop, the color and shape of your pubic hair, or your morning coffee routine—things tend to feel a little more personal. And when that relationship no longer works for you, there are a number of ways you can end things.

Even if you think this person depends heavily on your for cash or comfort, it's not your responsibility to be their cash cow or comfy chair. Returning to the same person because you feel obligated to help them can stop you from discovering other fabulous people you have yet to meet. Without being able to try new services (and the people who provide them), you are denying yourself a chance to find the best fit. While you may feel bad that you're no longer going to be the financial support for your eighteen-year-old dog walker, you don't have to keep hiring her so you can make sure that while she cleans up your dog's shit, you clean up hers. Ultimately, it's about what you need to do to help yourself most.

Each break up may be different, but the end result is the same. And you have the same options as breaking up with any other relationship, whether that be end it face-to-face, over the phone, through email, text or by disappearing.

As you end a relationship with someone whose job it is to help you, check in with yourself before you completely check out on them. For example, with a therapist or even a personal trainer, ask yourself if

DEAL BREAKERS

Not sure if you're on the outs with your doctor or your dog walker? Check out this list of definitive deal breakers when it comes to relationships of all shapes and sizes.

- You spend too much time and energy thinking about this person.
- You are too concerned about what this person thinks.
- You are constantly annoyed, angry, or hurt about something this person said or did.
- You aren't getting anything out of the relationship any longer.
- You feel like you're doing more therapy than your therapist or you have to go home and fix your hair after a haircut.
- You dread having to see this person, and you dream of never having to see them again.

you are setting realistic goals and meeting them. Have you finished the work you set out to do? Are they pushing your buttons because they're trying to help and you're interpreting this help as hurting you?

You also want to think about your comfort level around these people. When you go to meet with them, what feelings do they conjure up in you? Is it warmth? Do you get nervous? Nauseous? Does your body tingle or tighten up? Once you identify the feelings, figure out where they are coming from when you feel them. Is it your stomach? Chest? Head? All of this can help better explain how you're actually feeling, versus what you're thinking.

And not only can it help you explain how you feel, it also can help you put into words the reasons you don't want to be around them.

Once you decide you are ready to stop feeling the things you don't like, or to just stop being around someone you're not fond of, you can make a plan of action.

Only you can define when a relationship is relevant enough that it warrants an official undoing. And once you do, it's up to you to decide how to set everyone free (meaning you and the person you're dumping). The reality is, most of the time we are going to take the easy way out and just let this type of relationship go the way of the Western Black Rhinoceros (however unfortunate that may be). However, you don't want to deal with the stress of an accidental meeting at the market, or you just want to achieve bonus communication points in this lifetime or are into practicing the art of letting people go, have a break up conversation so you can learn how to express yourself clearly, and worry less about unplanned encounters. Here are three options for those ready to break up.

OPTION ONE: IMMEDIATE AND HONEST

Some relationships end quickly, and the break ups are easy. No offence is taken, and life goes on. There's generally a mutual understanding about what is causing the relationship to end (be it distance, differences of opinion, or some other way out). But sometimes things aren't easy, and that can make it challenging to be honest.

Being honest isn't something we have much practice with as a society. We get the message that it's easier to be nice than to be truthful. It helps us to look good and make another person feel good.

But practicing honesty can be a wonderful tool for learning how to communicate more effectively and learning how to hear feedback better. When you can be honest, especially in the moment after something has just transpired, you may feel lighter, because you were free to get things off your chest. Being honest doesn't mean you have to tell them every detail either. It just means you have to genuinely let them know why the relationship is ending.

For example, you go to get a haircut and you don't like it, and you're able to tell your hairdresser how you feel immediately after it happens. You may say something like, "I'm not sure that this cut is what I wanted, but it's the cut I have. I need to go home and sit with it for a night. If it's not what I like, I'm going to find someone else to change it for me. I hope you understand." Or, "I think at this point I'm too emotionally charged to come back to you."

When you can't actually tell them flat-out that you don't want to see them again, you can give them reasons as to why it's ending. Maybe they're good reasons too, like you've lost your job or your financial situation has changed. Perhaps you point out they showed up late the last three appointments, and you feel like they aren't respecting your time. Whatever route you go, finding a way to let someone know they can't meet your needs, or you theirs, is going to help them better understand why the relationship is ending.

This is also great for when you are terminating service with a medical professional. If you happen to be in the office and you know you're not coming back, telling them why can be really helpful. Especially if you are leaving as a result of something their staff did, they probably want to know what happened. Being honest about what went down can help them in the future. So, tell them if you don't like the wait time or their medical assistant; this way, they can try to enforce positive changes. You don't have to say much after that. You're not obligated to see them again, but giving them feedback is a valuable tool for better service.

♦ 🔒 ♦

Real-Life Break Ups

"I was dumped by my dermatologist. We parted ways because we were just too different. Despite the commonalities that kept us together so long, our generational contrast was too much.

For instance: I require the Internet to accomplish nearly everything. There is not one of my jobs I could do without it. Or at least, it would take at least three times as long. My dermatologist, on the other hand, does not appear to have digitized medical records, a website, or, as far as I saw, a professional email address.

We also have different ideas about the nature of the doctor-patient relationship. While I want to like my doctor, I don't need to be friends with them. I don't think the inner workings of my personal life are relevant to every medical visit. Other folks, many of whom are older than I, prefer to be treated by someone they know well. They build trust while having conversations at routine visits.

I was by far the youngest person I saw in my ex-dermatologist's office, and also apparently the only one who had a tight schedule. Not only did all his patients show up on time, some got there super early and chilled in the waiting room, enjoying (evidently) the slow jams and power ballads crackling through the speakers. It was also apparent that I was alone in my desire to be in and out without a lot of conversation. In what is probably a total coincidence, I had to wait about an hour for every five-minute visit.

After nearly four years, this disconnect on the usage of time came to a head. I asked about creative options for getting me in and out faster. They suggested I look for another office that could meet my needs and mailed me a 1993 Ann Landers column about why doctors are always running late. I was grateful someone had called it quits before there was bad blood.

To my dermatologist, I'm an impatient and entitled millennial who wants everything right this second. But to us—the kids who were raised on technological efficiency and who are forced, by economic realities created by baby boomers, to ceaselessly hustle at a series of part-time jobs to pay for student loans we were told would be the key to a stable financial future—[baby boomers] are the inconsiderate ones who don't understand our needs as patients or how critical timeliness is in a job market saturated with overeducated, underemployed talent.

What it came down to was that our generations have different values, different ideas of polite, and we are offended by different things. To get over it, I made an appointment with someone else. Hello, rebound!" —Timaree, story originally published in *Philadelphia Weekly*[1]

🔒

Yes, this takes courage, but even if it doesn't go as planned, you get credit for trying. And it may be the best bit of honest feedback these people have ever received. They may even appreciate it enough that they ask for one more chance to make things right. And they may not. Either way, there's something raw, naked, and beautiful about honesty.

OPTION TWO: TAKE YOUR TIME

Some relationships end gradually. Because you keep the relationship going, this type of break up often becomes long and drawn out. You may dance around the issue, taking small steps forward, But without having a clear idea of when you'll end this dying relationship, it can go on for months if not years. This can put you in a bind, but it also allows you to bide your time.

This is a good plan of action for when you still need help but you're not happy with the help you're getting. Instead of kicking your kid's babysitter to the curb, you either cut hours or days as you continue auditioning new help. And when you do find someone new, give the old babysitter two weeks' notice, or at least two weeks' pay. After all, it is a job, and that's proper etiquette for job termination. You can leave on a high note by offering to be a reference for future work.

It doesn't have the impact of a clean break, but it allows you to slowly break away from the person you're dealing with without simply cutting them out of your life. This is a good option with a trainer you see every day. While you may not want to end your exercise regime entirely, you may scale back from five days to twice a week. From there you can go biweekly, to once a month, to not at all.

With these relationships, it's important to be clear about your schedule. Give as much advanced notice as you can so they don't feel left in a lurch. This allows them a chance to find a new client, or plan what they will do with their soon-to-be free time.

So how does this go down? Okay, the next time you're scheduled to see your therapist, if you're ready to end therapy, then tell them. Therapists have a particular way they like to "terminate" a relationship, so they'll likely want to negotiate a finite number of sessions with you. This is how they wrap things up. Your therapist may suggest four sessions, but if you want to be out in one or two, you call the shots. He or she may not agree with your decision, but they can't force you to stay.

OPTION THREE: THE BLINDSIDED BREAK UP

Not all break ups go as planned, so it's better to plan to go with the break up as it unfolds. For example, just when you think you're breaking up with your therapist, he or she may turn the tables on you. "My break up with my therapist triggered the same physical and very similar emotional reactions to a romantic break up," says Aiisa, a friend of mine on Facebook. "While she had been all about being vulnerable, being authentic, having a connection, and resonating, when I expressed that I felt I wasn't seeing results and didn't feel like I had progressed to where I would like to be at that point in time, she basically said that she didn't want to see me anymore."

You may have to deal with the emotional reactions of someone you thought was trained to handle your emotions. Or when you tell your caregiver that you are letting them go, they may just up and leave weeks before you're actually ready for them to pack their bags.

If the break up doesn't go as planned, be prepared to roll with the punches. Have a list of additional therapists, caretakers, or other service providers available so that even if you are caught off guard, you're still on your game.

Saying Thank You

If the relationship ends on good terms, there are two ways to say thank you to a service provider. One requires you have disposable income, and one does not. If you do have a comfortable cash flow, a bonus on the last day can go a long way in showing your appreciation for their being a part of your child's life or your house's upkeep. Even if you didn't really click with them on a personal level, acknowledging them on a professional level shows you are a class act.

If you don't have the money, or they don't deserve it, you can write a note. Especially if you don't have the heart to go into the hair salon after the last worst haircut you'll ever get, mail a thank-you note to your former hairdresser. Sending a small note of appreciation for all the ways they didn't screw up allows them to feel good about the relationship. And then let them know that you're moving on and why. While it may be a little shocking to get a note of thanks that also acts as a break up letter, it will be less horrific if you run into them in another time and place. And they may even appreciate the notice.

All You Can Do Is Have a Plan

There is no perfect formula for breaking up. And while you don't need a reason to do so, you owe it to everyone involved to be as present and honest during the break up as you can be. How a relationship ends can determine how certain situations will go down in the future. While you can't predict how the break up will transpire, you can help choose your own adventure.

Running away from a break up will mean you will possibly have to run away from the person if you see ever them again. But confronting the end of an "other" relationship can make it easier to instead say hello and ask how they're doing. Taking your time to find a replacement while slowly working someone out of your life can allow you the space to move on naturally and afford you the opportunity to still have this person in your life in another capacity.

For example, when things end with understanding and compassion, you can consider inviting your kid's former nanny to his birthday parties if he still asks about her. You can refer your doctor to a friend (even if he or she wasn't right for you) and continue to shop in the same outlet mall you're former hairdresser still cuts hair in. Without closure of some kind, you might be cutting yourself off from these options.

We all make mistakes, and we can learn a lot from them. Breaking up with people doesn't always go as planned, but nothing does. And sometimes it's better to have a plan and see it through than walk away just because you can.

CONSIDERATIONS FOR THE BROKEN UP

1. This break up may come as a surprise, but don't let the element of the unexpected stop you from hearing what is being said.
2. Examine your part in the relationship and how it unraveled.
3. Just because you didn't work out for one person doesn't mean you won't work for other people in his or her circle.
4. It's okay to feel upset or angry, but don't try to invalidate their story.
5. Thank the other person for his or her honesty.

ELEVEN

Being Broken Up With: The Other Side of the Same Coin

Whether you saw it coming or not, being broken up with can be a tough pill to swallow. Not only is it a blow to your fragile ego-system, but it can come as a complete and total shock. It may not make any sense, or it may take some time for you to make sense of it, but you've been dumped, thrown out, released from your duty as a friend, family member, physician, or bandmate.

And it sucks. There's no candy-coating it. It's not fun to be rejected by someone you once had a relationship with—especially someone you hadn't really thought about breaking up with. It's not fun to be told you are now being discharged. But it happens. And while you may make a big deal of it (if for no other reason than because you can), one day, you may realize this person represents a small part of your life, and they are not the only person who ever mattered to you. A break up can give you a glimpse into the bigger picture and the person you are, or at the very least the person others see you as.

On the flip side, being the one broken up with can sometimes be easier. You won't have to beat yourself up about whether or not to stay, or figure out how you would end the relationship. You don't have to be the one going back and forth about what to do. Even though it hurts, you are not the only one hurting. For the person who broke up with you, the hurt likely started long before you broke up and may continue long after it's said and done.

It's not often a fast decision when someone chooses to end a relationship, just as it's not often an easy decision to accept that ending. Throughout this book, at the end of most chapters, I've offered tidbits of hope and help, so you can try to deal with your own situation better.

We all need reassurance when it comes to feeling good about our lives and ourselves. Whether we get that in school via good grades or through friends who love us, for most of us, we want to perceive ourselves as good people with good intentions.

The term "winning the break up" involves getting over the break up before the other person gets over you. It includes not calling, texting, or looking despondent when you run into your ex-bestie. It involves deleting your ex-business partner from your online life and moving on.[1] While this chapter isn't about winning the break up, it is about feeling like a winner again in your own life. You can do a spite dance, conjure up a curse for how they've made you feel, or huff and puff until you blow their house down, but none of these things are really going to make you feel better. So, what can you do to win even when you feel like you've lost?

How Field Goals Can Help You Stay Strong through a Break Up

If you are of the mindset that being broken up with means you fail at relationships, then it's more likely you will fail at relationships. Research confirms you may have the tendency to kick yourself when you're down. A 2009 study by Purdue University's Jessica Witt and Travis Dorsch found that performance influences perception.[2]

Using field goals as a marker for determining how perception impacts a football player's kicking performance, the Purdue team chose a group of non-professional players and asked them to kick field goals. They found those who failed to kick field goals believed the goal posts were too close together to get the ball through. And the larger the "players" perceived the distance between goal posts, the more field goals they actually kicked. In layman's terms, people who see the bigger picture score more goals.

This is an interesting reminder about the process of breaking up. Any break up is a pretty big deal. Both of you are gaining independence from a situation that has been holding you back (whether you realized it or not). If you can perceive yourself as the Incredible Hulk or Popeye post-spinach, or if you feel like you have a large support network to help you get by, you will likely do well in your break up. If you have a can-do attitude, you are more likely to have the physical and mental strength and ability to get over the break up.

But if you envision yourself more like Superman holding kryptonite or think of yourself as completely alone and unfriendable, then you will not only be weak in the break up, but you will also feel totally isolated and unlikeable. That's because when your perception is weak, it's easier to get sucked back into feelings of being bad or wrong and thinking the break up was "your fault."

By seeing the bigger picture, you can learn how to perform at your best through a break up. You will not see the end of this relationship as insurmountable. You won't continue to fail, because you will believe you can succeed. If you tell yourself the end of this relationship will change your life for the better, you will already be on the road to a better life. And because your perception impacts your performance, having the foresight to see the good in the bad can help you face the break up with confidence and courage.

And there's also that other bit of research out of Amsterdam, the

WANT TO FEEL BETTER?

Need some help dealing with the break up blues? Try these actions:

Stay off social media. If someone you see on Facebook or other social media sites breaks up with you, remove yourself from their online presence. Seeing their daily whereabouts will make it harder to accept the situation and can also make you feel bad about not being a part of their life. Don't recieve mutual friends' updates. This way, you don't potentially run into a post about them, or a photo of them having a good time out with other people you know. If you never want to see what they're up to, you have the option of blocking them for good.

Get out of bed. Even if you already do this to go to work, you need to do this even when you have no other plans. It may mean walking to the store to get a bag of potato chips or going out clubbing to dance it off. Whatever your preferred method of leaving your house or apartment, get out. The more you are living, the less time you'll have for loathing.

See a therapist. It can help to talk with someone outside of your social circle. A therapist, or other counselor, is a perfect choice for helping you get over the feelings about being broken up with. These types of people can help you find the lessons in the relationship, as well as give you tools and techniques for coping.

Write a letter, and never mail it. If you feel like you didn't get the closure you desired, then writing a letter to your "ex-bestie" can be pretty cathartic. It can be a meaningful exercise and give you a chance to articulate what you are feeling and get it out of your system. You

➜

can make a copy of the letter and leave it in an envelope in a drawer, then plan on revisiting it in a few months. This way you can see how much of what you're feeling still rings true. And if you're over it before then, you can always burn it in a ceremonial fire.

Stay busy. Now is the time to fill up your social calendar. Make plans. Go on dates. Take a vacation. Doing whatever you can do to keep yourself occupied, with the intention of having a good time, is a good thing. This way, your brain doesn't become your own worst enemy.

Meditate or exercise. Keeping your body and brain healthy is a good way to keep the rest of you healthy too.

study that points to how our bodies make a big deal physically about break ups (see Chapter One). So, try telling yourself that your heart is making you feel like this is a bigger deal than it actually is, and you might be able to keep things straight in your head. Because, despite the things your brain and body are telling you, these sensations and thoughts are only temporary.

Any way you look at it, science proves break ups impact our sense of self-worth and well-being. And that's okay, it happens. But when you can move on and understand the process, you can kick some major field goals.

Getting Past the Blame Game

If you can look at the break up from the point of view of the other person in the equation, do you see how hard it can be to initiate it? Can you think of how many times you've initiated a break up in your life? Or did you usually wait for someone else to make the first move?

It's really tough to actually break up with someone. It takes courage and conviction to be able to say how you feel and to stand your ground. Breaking up is not done for sport. It's generally a serious deci-sion to end a relationship with someone you care about. Even when you do the breaking up, you can be uncertain. The breaker upper may have his or her doubts about whether or not they've done the right thing (unless the relationship was so bad, or abusive, that neither of you doubt the decision). They will be sad and happy, missing you and reminiscing too.

The question remains, how are you doing? You may be experienc-ing a sense of loss, but also a sense of relief. You may be angry, hurt, or feeling abandoned. You may want to blame your aches and pains on the person who dumped you. But, even if you do, they are still your aches and pains to soothe.

If you can get past feeling like something bad has been done to you, then you can start to see some good in all of this too. By blaming someone else for your feelings, you are actually doing yourself more harm than good. You give away your power. You lose any sense of con-trol you may have in the situation. You could have done the breaking up too, but you chose not to. Still, that doesn't mean you weren't feeling that something needed to change. You have the ability to move on and woman up. But if you continue to blame someone else for your feelings, you have no power at all.

Even if you think it's going to help you to blame them in the short term, blame is more like fresh cement than sustenance. Once you get stuck in the idea that you have been wronged, you will have a harder time feeling like you will be all right.

And if you continue to blame others, you can't learn to move on. You can't see what you may have done to be broken up with. You will continue to feel like a victim. And this can be just like seeing the smaller goal posts in lieu of the wider angle.

When you can hold your dumper accountable for her specific actions around the relationship and the break up instead of blaming her for everything that went wrong, you can feel powerful, confident, and in control. Blame is about punishment, while accountability is about exploring the roles you both played in the relationship. You may not agree with how things happened, but blaming is a childish way of making sense of a situation. Accountability is more adult.

You can turn the situation around by taking care of your needs and feelings. Self-care goes a long way in letting you be the best friend you need right now. Also find support from others who love you, or simply like you.

The Benefits of Being Broken Up With

I know it's hard to hear things like, "It's for the best," or, "It will get better," but people effectively use these phrases all the time as coping mechanisms for moving on. And even if it's not for the best, because it sucks not to have this person in your life anymore, you have to hope that it will get better. Especially since that's the only option (right now). If someone feels you're not good and healthy for their life anymore, then they weren't great for your life either.

Through all the anger, tears, resentment, joy, or whatever emotion you're currently feeling, there are benefits to being broken up with. The more we remember this, the more likely we are to be able to move forward with the picture of a happy, smiley emoticon in our head.

BE HONEST WITH YOURSELF

I grew up hearing the phrase "Honesty is the best policy." And, even when it hurts, it generally rings true. When someone breaks up with you, they are being honest about how the relationship feels to them, and they are taking the time to take care of themselves. Now it's time for you to try to do the same. How honest can you be with yourself? Is it a relief to finally know where you stand? How does it feel to be out of the gray area and moved into a place where things are black and white?

Think about it. You don't have to worry about figuring out if you're in a good or bad place with this person anymore, because you aren't in their space at all. And that means you don't have to worry about saying, or doing, something wrong. Also, it can be a comfort to

THE SCAPEGOATING SOCIETY

Ever heard of the Scapegoating Society? It was founded in 1997 as a resource both for people who have been forced to bear the blame for others and for people who work professionally to prevent this very thing from happening. If you are transferring all the blame and responsibility of this break up onto the other person, you may want to check them out. And even if they don't make you feel better, being aware of what you're doing is a good way to stop doing it.[4]

know—quite possibly for the first time in the relationship—you have been given an honest, accurate assessment of what is going on. Even if you hate them for it, you can admire their honesty. Yes?

REFLECTION AND INSIGHT

Looking back on the relationship, you can learn a lot by taking the time to answer some questions you may not have thought about while you were in the relationship. For example, what was your role in the relationship? (I.e., were you manipulating or manipulated? Did you give in or give up?) Do you have a "type" of persona you can identify with? (I.e., victim, drama queen, protagonist, servant, warlord?) Who caused the arguments and who reinforced this conditioning? Did you feel like you were treated with respect for your opinions and beliefs? What did you agree and disagree on?

A break up is a great chance for reflection, so look at the roles you assigned to each other and analyze your part in the "performance."

Sure, a relationship isn't a play, but you get the picture. Reflection leads to insight. And it gives you a chance to assess what types of people you want to be around. If your ex-boss was a conservative Republican and you're an anarchist, perhaps you now know you can't work with people with a certain types of political beliefs. Maybe that's you're trigger. Or, maybe you can work with them, but you need to think about how to better handle the situation the next time around.

SEEING THE POSITIVE SIDE OF CHANGE

You now have the opportunity to do you. You got broken up with, and you can't change that, at least not right now. But what you can do, if you choose to accept this quest, is find ways this past relationship can help you to implement positive changes in your life. For example, look at the actions you took with regard to your ex. How could you have made things better during the relationship, or even through the break up? If there are things you can change for the better, how far are you willing to go to make these changes? And if you do make those changes, will you feel better about yourself?

NO MORE ENERGY SUCK

Bad relationships often have vampire-like energy, draining a lot from you, sometimes without you even realizing it. But once it's over and you don't have to think about the problems in that relationship any longer, you can stop using your energy to "deal" with this person.

After the break up, you may notice an energy shift. Feel the effects of no longer having to focus your thoughts and energy on someone who wasn't always making you act like your best self. You now have time to focus your energy on new things, like your life, making new friends, and enjoying new activities.

Along with the shift in energy, you now have the opportunity to shift your focus elsewhere. What will you do, and where will you go?

IT'S ABOUT GROWTH

You may see the ending of this non-romantic relationship as a failure, but actually, it's an opportunity. Even if you remember the relationship as all good before it turned bad, there was obviously room for improvement. In terms of growth, make a list of the ways you grew from, and in, the relationship. Just because it had to end doesn't mean the good parts of the relationship have to go away. There is value in taking the good with the bad and then using all of it to grow.

"FREEDOM IS ANOTHER WORD FOR NOTHING LEFT TO LOSE"

Ultimately, breaking up is not all "happy, happy, joy, joy." But you have to admit there is an element of relief from being set free. Understanding you are the only one responsible for your feelings can be quite freeing. If you can let go of the feelings of being burned, scorned, and one-upped, you can create space for feeling other things. And you can begin to look inside yourself and probe around to find the things you enjoy feeling. You will realize you are free to let go of this relationship and pursue other avenues now.

On top of that, you are still alive. And you (hopefully) have a lot of life left in you. You too get to choose the relationships you have in your life and get rid those you don't want anymore. You are lucky you live in a time when and place where you aren't being told what to do, how to think, or how to act. So embrace this newfound opportunity. Go out there and live your life!

HOW TO EXCEL AT BEING BROKEN UP WITH

"Living well is the best revenge. So is out living them."

"Pick a D. C.—designated contactee. Every time you feel compelled to call, email, or text the person who dumped you, you contact your D. C. instead. Tell your D. C. anything and everything you need to say to the dumper. You get it off your chest and walk away without saying things you will regret."

"I don't suppose 'lots of booze, pot, crying, music, and lost weekends' would be an acceptable response. I just know it's worked for me."

"Go to work. Don't let it fester."

"Self-care, eat well, sleep well, journal, stay busy, and take time for yourself, plus allow yourself to grieve. Allowing the contradictions is important. The longing and loss as well as moving on."

"Karma will take care of it all. It may take time, but eventually it happens."

"Let go!"

"Think of it as a gift. You've been released from a relationship that was failing to satisfy the needs of both partners. It's an opportunity for growth and self-discovery each time."

"Pretend you are happy and okay until you are. (Which sounds like terrible advice, but it works somehow)."

"You cry and feel pain and heartbreak and that is okay. Just remember those feelings are only temporary and you will feel better in the future."

"Work out. Sweat. Perspire."

"I always found that taking a trip somewhere that I had never been was a great way to get myself moving forward. And 'success is the best revenge' helped me focus more on the future than the past."

TWELVE

Navigating the Aftermath

You've ended it. It's over. And whether you feel like dancing in your underwear à la Tom Cruise in *Risky Business* or sitting around talking to your computer like Joaquin Phoenix does in the movie *Her*, you are responsible for how you choose to embrace the final scene in this relationship drama.

Sometimes the hardest part of a break up is making the break, and sometimes that's only the beginning of the hurt. It may not be something you're prepared for, definitely not fully, and aftercare can be surprisingly difficult, even if the break up is a "good thing."

You are likely experiencing a wide range of emotions. Feelings you weren't planning on having may begin to surface. There's probably some relief associated with the fact that you went through with the break up. You may feel angry about being put in a situation where breaking up seemed like the only option or about how it all went down. You may be experiencing sadness for what you have lost or happiness about what you are gaining (a greater understanding of self-care and your own self-worth).

Mourning a loss via break up may feel worse than if the person you broke up with were actually dead. And that's because they're not dead. Their life goes on without you. But your life goes on without them too.

Because break ups can be emotional rollercoasters, aftercare is super important. It allows us a chance to prioritize our own needs and show ourselves that love, positivity, and the desire to get better are things that help us move forward. Aftercare carves out a space for mourning and reflection. It's a chance to look back at the relationship and make sense of our role in the story. It gives us a way to get creative and express ourselves better, and it provides us the room we need to grow. On the other end of aftercare is a newfound freedom to be truer to ourselves and to enjoy more good relationships in our life.

Take a moment to give yourself credit for going through the break up, whether you feel like you handled it well, poorly, or somewhere in between. Because going through the break up took a lot, and now you are breaking on through to the other side.

" *Do not expect to get from the break up what you did not get from the relationship. You can't break up with somebody as a move to try to make him or her change. It's not sustainable.* **"**
—MARCIA BACZYNSKI, RELATIONSHIP COACH

Getting Over the Humps

You have to engage your mind and body in getting over a break up. You'll need to continue to work on moving forward until it becomes a natural act. You have to think yourself to a place where everything is going to be all right, sometimes months before you actually get there. When you come to a place of understanding the situation, or accepting you will never completely comprehend how it all went down, then you are slowly getting over the hump. From there you can decide if you're going to move on to a place of freedom, forgiveness, forgetting, or "fuck you."

YOU ARE WHERE YOU ARE

Welcome to the here and now. Whether you feel invigorated by the break up or as if you're actually broken, when you can accept where you are, you can just be there. Even if you're the kind of person who thinks a lot (I am) and sometimes finds that beating yourself up feels pretty comforting (I do), when you stop beating yourself up, you can just be.

It's not easy, but it's simple. It doesn't take a lot to just say, "I'm here right now," or whatever words work for you. And if it's not a place you want to be, then it's okay to work toward going other places. You'll get there in your own time or you won't.

YOU AREN'T BROKEN

You are not the only person who has ever broken up with a family member, a friend, or a business partner. Yes, you may feel alone. Yes, you may feel angry or sad. Odds are, you'll get over it. Right now, you need to remember there's nothing wrong with you, and you are strong (which has been proven by the fact that you took action around the break up). You are not broken; you are fixed.

FEEL IT

No matter what you're feeling, it's important to feel it. Whether your emotions make you feel like you're flying on top of the world or barely breathing at the bottom of the sea, you want to explore all of your feelings. Scream into a pillow, or get some of your best feelings out on paper. Try meditation or some other form of self-expression. However you choose to handle the loss, it is a loss and your emotions needs to be dealt with. If you can feel your way through your break up, you will be able to be more honest about how you're doing.

Check in with your body. How does it feel? Do you feel lighter without the burden of this other situation (and person/people) riding on your back? Are your muscles tense? Do you feel a sense of freedom that's allowing your limbs to move more loosely? Are you ready to find the highest hill and sing "The Sound of Music" from its peak?

Or are you surprised that it feels like you had the wind knocked out of you? Are you devastated about the end of the relationship? Have you fallen down a pit of despair so deep you don't know how you're going to climb out?

Maybe you're somewhere in between, teetering on the edge of euphoria and depression. Of course you can be nowhere near either extreme, instead just moving along in your life, doing it in your own time and at your own pace.

Wherever you find yourself, there's no map that gives you the most direct mourning strategy. If any of these feelings become obstacles, you will find ways to get through them. Feelings are all temporary, even the ones we wish could last forever. Remember that, and use some other tools to help you get by. Whether that means talking to a therapist, doing yoga, getting out of your house so you can get out of your head, or listening to your favorite band, you can navigate your way over and around the humps by facing your feelings.

FOLLOW YOUR GUT

Intuition is an amazing thing. It's free, and it generally speaks loud and clear. It's something we should try to listen to because we know it's right. It reminds us that only we know what's best for us. While this or any book, person, or podcast can tell us how we "should" feel, we are the only person who knows how we really feel.

Listen to your gut; it really is telling you something. It doesn't mean you can't ask for opinions or advice, but it does mean any advice or opinions you ask for should be processed through your internal system. Hear your heart, but listen to your gut. Because while the heart wants what it wants, your gut knows what is best for you.

So, as you move through the break up, reflect inward. What is going on inside of you? What is your instinctual animal self telling you? How does what your brain says differ from what your heart wants? If you can tap into your "organ"ic relationship, you will find you are in the best position to help yourself. That may sound exhausting, and it may sound exhilarating. You get to decide.

CREATE TIME-LIMITED OBSESSING

After a relationship ends, there is usually a certain amount of time we spend obsessing over its demise. To help you get over the part where you constantly beat yourself up, marriage and family therapist Dr. Sheri Meyers advises going on an "Obsession Diet."[1] To do so, she recommends allotting yourself a set amount of time (i.e. five minutes per hour) when you can throw yourself into the negative feelings the break up is causing. Set your timer, and once five minutes is up, your obsessing is over until the next hour. Each day you reduce the time. So if you start at five minutes, then you go to four, to three, and you get the picture.

Not only is this a good way to learn you are in control of your thoughts, but you are also still giving yourself permission, as well as the time and space, to have said thoughts.

You can also practice time-limited obsessing by actually throwing yourself a pity party. Invite over some of your closest friends, and have one night where you get to cry if you want to (after all, it is your party). Have friends bring you gifts that can take your mind off of the break up, like board games or offers to hang out, and create a sign-in book where guests write inspirational messages and suggest fun activities. And then, even after your pity party is over, you have a resource of helpful words and activities to move you through this challenging time.

CONJURE UP A CLEARING RITUAL

It may sound too hippie-dippie for you, but it can be nice to take a specific action to clear out old energy. On a vacation on an island off an island (yeah, I was pretty remote), a friend and I made a sacred circle to help me get past the sadness of a friendship break up. As part of our ritual, we saged each other as well as the circle we had created.

I saw it as a way to acknowledge that I needed to move forward.

I used the sage as a symbolic object to help guide me toward clearer thinking. It was also an act symbolic of freeing myself from the thoughts that were beating me down.

If saging isn't your thing, you can still find a ritual that is. Perhaps it's taking all the old photos of you and your ex-bestie and burying them in your backyard. Or maybe it's cleaning your house so you can remove any leftover bad energy from the last time your sister-in-law visited. If you've broken up with a business partner, it could be burning all your old documents (assuming you won't be needing them).

A clearing ritual can give you something to reflect on. It can be a way to remember that you are free to go and do your own thing.

IT'S ABOUT LOVE

In her book *Love 2.0*, Dr. Barbara L. Fredrickson explains how non-romantic love is important for human growth and survival. She writes, "Love is the essential nutrient that your cells crave: true positivity-charged connection with other living beings."[2]

Love is like sunshine: we need it to grow and be healthy. And now that you have even more room for love in your life, you can grow bigger and stronger. Yippee!

Hear the Music

Music has the power to move us in many ways. It can heal us with its melodies and change our mood in an instant. Are there certain songs that make you feel like you can take over the world, or that at least move you into a good emotional place? Make your own playlist of songs that lift you up and listen to it every time you're feeling down.

Don't Think About the Unbreaking Up Part (Yet)

It's challenging to keep your mind from wandering to the hope of reconciliation with the person you are broken up with. Even if you hate them right now, you may have an instant reaction to the fact they are no longer around by needing them around more. (Like cupcakes

BREAK UP PLAYLIST

Need help compiling a post–break up playlist? Here's a thirty-song feel-good-post-break up playlist I created with some help from my friends.

1. "Survivor" — Destiny's Child
2. "Happy" — Pharrell Williams
3. "Hayling" — FC Kahuna
4. "Feeling Good" — Nina Simone
5. "Freedom '90" — George Michael
6. "Back to Black" — Amy Winehouse
7. "Shake It Out" — Florence + The Machine
8. "Albert's Shuffle" — Mike Bloomfield & Al Kooper
9. "I Will Survive" — either the Gloria Gaynor or CAKE version
10. "Fistful of Love" — Antony and the Johnsons
11. "Wake Up" — Arcade Fire
12. "Don't Think Twice It's Alright" — Bob Dylan
13. "I'm Not Crying" — Flight of the Conchords

on day one of a diet.) Or you may wish that they could just change this one thing they do that really pisses you off. You could be dreaming of the time when this can be all behind you and you can both see the errors of your ways. We all want things to go well in our lives, and sometimes the break up is what puts us back on track.

Before you can get to that place of moving forward, you have to get past the place of hurt. Time is such a necessary part of the healing process, and only after a significant amount of time has passed can you decide your next steps with clarity.

While it's generally not advisable in romantic relationships, in non-romantic relationships, people can, and do, reconnect later

14. "Fighter" — Christina Aguilera

15. "Groove Is in the Heart" — Deee-Lite

16. "Thrift Shop" — Macklemore & Ryan Lewis (feat. Wanz)

17. "Beautiful Day" — U2

18. "Shake it Off" — Taylor Swift

19. "Your Ex-Lover Is Dead" — The Stars

20. "Solsbury Hill" — Peter Gabriel

21. "Somebody That I Used to Know" — Gotye (feat. Kimbra) Tiesto Remix

22. "Rolling in the Deep" — Adele

23. "I'll Rise" — Ben Harper & The Innocent Criminals

24. "You Get What You Give" — New Radicals

25. "It's My Life" — Bon Jovi

26. "Loser" — Beck

27. "Boom Boom Pow" — The Black Eyed Peas

28. "Don't Stop Believin'" — Journey

29. "We Found Love" — Rihanna feat. Calvin Harris

30. "Run the World (Girls)" — Beyoncé

on—especially close friends and family members. If you get back together after a break up, things are generally better, or at least different than before the two of you took a break. A reconnected relationship can mean the connection is less enmeshed (which is a good thing when the drama was high) or more casual. But a break up doesn't mean you can't have relationship 2.0. It all depends on what happens when you have some time and distance.

I have reconnected with two ex-friends and one family member, and two out of those three times, the relationship got better after the break. In the third situation, the relationship was just different. We were no longer best friends—okay, we were barely friends—but to this day, we still enjoy catching up on the rare occasions that we see or hear from one another.

When it came to getting back together, it was never planned. It just happened when the time was right. And even though I was looking for a way back in, I wasn't expecting I would find it right away, if ever. There is no quick fix for a broken relationship, except to stay broken up. So, while it's fresh, keep the Band-Aid off and let the relationship hurt heal. Then see how you feel after your boo-boo is all better.

To Forgive or Not To Forgive— That Is the Question

" The weak can never forgive. Forgiveness is the attribute of the strong. "

—MAHATMA GANDHI

Forgiveness is ingrained in us, both as a religious and a cultural act, and we spend a great deal of time (and money) focused on asking for forgiveness. Catholics confess and repent around Easter. Jews ask for forgiveness at Yom Kippur. Bulgarians apologize on a day they call Sirni Zagovezni (Forgiveness Day). Walk into any drugstore, and there are whole sections of cards that say, "I'm sorry."

But what about forgiving? How often do we focus on that? When's the last time you saw a card that read, "I forgive you"?

In some cases, like abuse, you can't really ever forgive. (Or if you can, that's a topic for another book.) In most cases, forgiveness is challenging because we closely align it with forgetting. But in almost any situation, forgiveness isn't for them; it's about us. We don't even need to let the person know we forgive them; we just need to be able to forgive them in our heart, so that we can let go and move on.

Forgiving someone else may be one of the most difficult things you ever do. By forgiveness, I don't mean you necessarily have to forgive the person you're breaking up with for what went wrong, but it helps if you can forgive them for not being who you needed them to be.

You can't turn them into someone they're not, even though we often spend a lot of our energy trying to do just that. By forgiving them, we can let go of the expectations we held for them, and we can create new expectations for our lives.

Being able to accept another person's fallibility is a way to accept your own imperfections. We all make mistakes. When we can put ourselves in the position of the person who "screwed up," we can accept that we screw up too. This may help us to let go of some of the anger and pain we carry around with us.

Before you choose how and why to forgive, you can try asking yourself an essential, seemingly morbid, question: If the person you broke up with died tomorrow, would you be okay with how you let things end? Would you still be angry with them after they died? Or would you find a way to let them rest in peace? If you can get to a place of peace after they're gone, perhaps you can find a way to find peace for yourself while they're still alive.

If you're down to forgive (with no requirement to forget), you can try a program like Radical Forgiveness, which claims to help you get past relationship problems. I can't guarantee that it works, but if you have some extra spending money and you want to check it out, there are online programs on forgiving parents, siblings, children, and co-workers. I believe, in general, if you really want a program to work for you, then you can make it work.[3]

You can also do some sort of forgiveness ceremony, whether that means reciting something, releasing something, or dancing around your living room blasting Florence + The Machine's "Shake It Out." When you can find a way to forgive, silently or out loud, you are making life better for yourself.

“ *Forgiveness is for you, not anyone else. Think of forgiveness as a process, not a one-time event. It is necessary to forgive repeatedly, every time you think of the wrong done. It helps you heal and move past the hurt. Forgiveness does not mean that*

you don't want consequences for the person who hurt you, or
that you still want that person in your life. It just means that you
are stronger than that hurt and you are ready to take back the
power you have over your own thoughts and feelings. Is it nec-
essary for healing? I believe it is for complete healing. However,
people function well in life without forgiving, but they still carry
the pain of that wrong done. **"**

—Dr. Lisa Ann Powell, LMFT-S

Now, let's play devil's advocate here. When we don't forgive, we can place all the blame on the other person. And it's a lot easier to be angry with someone else than it is to be upset with ourselves. Why should we own our part of the problem, if they can't see the error of their ways? When we don't make it about us, we can make it about how they hurt us. And if someone hurt us, why should we ever forgive them?

Besides, if we forgive them, won't we forget how they hurt us? Sure, research out of Scotland[4] says that you are more likely to intentionally forget when you forgive. But depending on the seriousness of the transgression, does it matter if you forget, especially if it doesn't change the fact that the relationship is over?

Perhaps by intellectualizing the whole experience, you can forego forgiveness. You can accept them for who they are or aren't and not forgive them. Or you can forgive them but disapprove of their actions. But often times, when we sit with the pain, we continue to reopen the wound. And if we can't find a way to release the hurt, then the wound never properly heals.

If you prefer not to forgive, ask yourself why. Are you reminding yourself of their flaws and faults so you never let them back into your life? Hint: you can forgive them and still never let them back into your life. Or are you holding on to feelings of bitterness and resentment so you still have something of theirs to hold on to? Maybe it's just that you hate them and don't believe they deserve to be forgiven. There's no right answer, only your answer.

TO FORGIVE OR NOT FORGIVE: SPIRITUAL LEADERS ANSWER THE QUESTION

"I personally think that forgiveness is often overly empha-sized in this kind of language. Healing and forgiveness are not the same thing. A person can heal from terrible kinds of abuse and mistreatment without ever getting to a place of "forgiveness" of his/her abuser. When we put the emphasis on forgiveness too much, we run the risk of guilt-tripping someone who has suffered horribly at the hands of another, or making them feel insufficient, when it's not true that all crimes can engender forgiveness. Certainly, if an individual can get to a place of forgiveness—whether or not the one forgiven has ever exhibited any signs of penitence, willing-ness to change, or even awareness that s/he has done any-thing wrong—it can be important and liberating. But it's not a requirement—definitely not something the abused 'owes' the abuser, and not something that the abused is 'wrong' if s/he never gets to." —Rabbi Danya Ruttenberg

"Forgiveness is always necessary, but it's not always easy and it takes time. That said, not forgiving only hurts *you*. Resentment just keeps you locked in an evil and non-loving response." —Mike Hayes, spiritual director

"I think that forgiveness is important because if we carry anger inside of us, then it affects our body. The body is the place where we store feelings and emotions. It can also affect us spiritually, especially if you walk around resentful and therefore see things through that lens. That being said, forgiveness is *not* forgetting. You don't have to let someone treat you the same way again. That would be foolish. Still, it can often take a while for the anger and hurt to subside enough to begin the process of forgiving." —Rabbi Gary Katz

→

"I see forgiveness as something we do to set ourselves free. It has little to nothing to do with the other person and does not require an apology. As long as we refuse to forgive someone, we live and get stuck in the pain of the hurt or disappointment. Once we forgive, we feel lighter and can move forward. We also must remember that forgiving does not mean forgetting, and it does not mean the pain never happened. It just means that we honor our sense of peace and we accept that our present and future are more important than the past." —Tamara Horch-Prezioso, ordained minister, Reiki master, and intuitive counselor

Even with the downsides to forgiveness, the reality is that forgiveness is often a pick-me-up for the person who makes it happen. That being said, we all have different methods for moving on. Just because forgiveness seems like a good idea for some people doesn't mean it works for everyone. So, before you choose to forgive or not to forgive, figure out what works best for you. And although you never have to do it, if you choose to, do it for you.

On Regret

For many years, I had a quote stuck in my head, one that I had heard in the beginning of a song. It went, "I would rather regret something I did than something I didn't do."

I'm not sure who the original quote maker was, although I've seen it attributed to the fictional SNL character Jack Handey. But just like "Fear is joy paralyzed," these twelve words helped me out every time I began to feel like I had made a mistake in a relationship, or life in general. And to this day, when I start to doubt my decisions, I utter that phrase and remember I would rather regret taking a risk than playing it safe.

Breaking up with someone you care about, or you care enough

about to actually break up with, is taking a risk. You risk losing someone who has helped you grow, and you risk losing other people, or an entire community, as a result of cutting ties. After it's said and done, the broken-up-with may reject your words or treat you like something they would squash on the street. They may even try to turn it around, exclaiming that you are the problem and they are the solution. Whatever happens, you have made a decision, and you need to stick to it.

You won't know what you actually want, or how they will truly react, until you can step away from the situation. Only after the break up can you look back and understand what you had, or what you needed, and what it means to not have it any longer.

You are mourning a loss. If you're wallowing in regret over the decision, try working out, making art, hanging out with friends, throwing yourself a pity party, journaling, and taking a trip to get over the hump. If those don't work, just ride the wave of regret. And strap in. It will get bumpy.

Take Care

As this chapter, and this book, comes to a close, I hope you have felt a shared experience and connection around non-romantic break ups. Sure, break ups are different for every person and each situation; however, there is something universal in the fact that we all suffer loss and we have to deal with filling a void.

Maybe you turn to other friends, a husband or wife, or a new exercise routine after ending a long friendship. Perhaps you stop talking to your family for a while after you get rid of that sister who's been nagging you for decades. You may find another church after leaving yours, or you may decide that spirituality without religion is your thing. While there are no right answers, there are some things we can agree on. The most obvious one is that breaking up is hard, but that doesn't mean that it's not worth it.

Breaking up can be vital for your happiness, and it may also be vital for your health. Think of the process of ending a relationship in the same way you think about getting in shape. It takes time to see the results you've set out to achieve, and it may take smaller goals to help you get through the daily bump and grind. When it comes to getting healthy, you have to work regularly and be mindful of what you eat. While the work can be more difficult than sitting on the couch watching *The Long Island Medium*, the end results are way more worth it. Or, if you hate exercise and only eat junk food, try to think of breaking up like breathing. Sometimes, it's the only way to stay alive.

Whatever you do to take care of yourself after a relationship ends, take care of yourself. That means allowing yourself to acknowledge the break up and experiencing the emotions you are feeling. You can do this through writing, drawing, and talking out loud to yourself, your therapist, or your support network. You can feel better by reading more books or articles on the subject. You can get out and hike, camp, and travel. You may work on imparting a "yes, you can" attitude or changing something about your appearance, whether it's a haircut, shopping, or just relaxing your body by getting a massage. You may just need to sit on your couch and watch movies.

Life is the experience you make of it. Break ups are life's lessons about relationships and what works and what doesn't work for us. Break ups are about acceptance and accountability. They are about making space and holding your own space too.

Break ups hurt, and you have to heal. It takes a lot of the time to get over someone, and for a while, it may tap into your energy reserves. Still, it's a necessary part of our own evolution. And once you get over the hump, it can lead to new feelings of freedom and possibility.

How you handle a break up is going to impact *your* life more than it will impact anyone else's life. So choose wisely, choose thoughtfully, and, most of all, choose you.

Notes

CHAPTER ONE

1. Rachel Zarrell, "This Boston Marathon Survivor Wrote A Breakup Letter To Her Leg Before Amputating It," *Buzzfeed.com,* November 11, 2014, http://www.buzzfeed.com/rachelzarrell/adios-leg.

2. Timaree Schmit, "Timaree's Body: Why Is My Doctor Always Running Late?" *PhillyNow.com,* December 11, 2014, http://phillynow.com/2014/12/11/timarees-body-why-is-my-doctor-always-running-late/.

3. Kat George, "Why Ending A Friendship Is So Much Harder Than Ending A Romantic Relationship." *Bustle,* October 2014, http://www.bustle.com/articles/44167-why-ending-a-friendship-is-so-much-harder-than-ending-a-romantic-relationship.

4. Doka, K.J. Disenfranchised Grief: *A hidden sorrow.* (Lexington, MA: Lexington Books, 1989).

5. Bregtje Gunther Moor, Eveline A. Crone and Maurits W. van der Molen, "The Heartbrake of Social Rejection: Heart Rate Deceleration in Response to Unexpected Peer Rejection," *Psychological Science* 21, no. 9 (2010): 326-333, doi: 10.1177/0956797610379236.

6. S. Halpern-Meekin, W. D. Manning, P. C. Giordano, and M. A. Longmore, "Relationship Churning in Emerging Adulthood: On/Off Relationships and Sex With an Ex," *Journal of Adolescent Research* 28, no. 2 (2012): 166-188, doi: 10.1177/0743558412464524.

CHAPTER TWO

1. Robert Burns, "*To a Mouse, on Turning Her Up in Her Nest with the Plough.*"

2. Sandra Metts, "The Language of Disengagement: A Face-Management Perspective," in *Close Relationship Loss: Theoretical Approaches*, ed. Terri L. Orbuch. (New York: Springer, 1992), 111-127.

3. Tara J. Collins and Omri Gillath, "Attachment, breakup strategies, and associated outcomes: The effects of security enhancement on the selection of breakup strategies," *Journal of Research in Personality* 46, no. 2 (2012): 210-222, doi:10.1016/j.jrp.2012.01.008.

4. Michael Tomasello, *Why We Cooperate*. (Boston, The MIT Press, 2009).

5. (Marcia Baczynksi, pers.comm.)

CHAPTER THREE

1. Daniel Ploskin, MD, "What is codependence?, *PsychCentral*, 2013, http://psychcentral.com/lib/what-is-codependence/0001170.

2. Gregg Henriques, "Signs of counter-dependency," *Psychology Today*, April 2014, https://www.psychologytoday.com/blog/theory-knowledge/201404/signs-counter-dependency.

3. Darlene Lancer, "Codependency vs. Interdependency," *PsychCentral*, January, 2013, http://psychcentral.com/lib/codependency-vs-interdependency/00014263.

CHAPTER FOUR

1. S. Metts, W. R. Cupach, and R. A. Bejlovec, "'I love you too much to ever start liking you,' Redefining romantic relationships," *Journal of Social and Personal Relationships* 6, no. 3 (1989): 259–274, doi: 10.1177/0265407589063002.

CHAPTER FIVE

1. Lynne C. Giles, Glonek Gary F. V., Luszcz Mary A., and Andrews, Gary R, "Effect of social networks on 10 year survival in very old Australians: the Australian longitudinal study of aging," *Journal of*

Epidemiol Community Health 59, no. 7 (2005): 574-579, doi:10.1136/jech.2004.025429.

2. Fatih Ozbay, MD; corresponding author Douglas C. Johnson, PhD; Eleni Dimoulas, PhD; C.A. Morgan, III, MD, MA; Dennis Charney, MD; and Steven Southwick, MD, "Social Support and Resilience to Stress. From Neurobiology to Clinical Practice," *Psychiatry* 4, no. 5 (2007): 35–40, http://www.ncbi.nlm.nih.gov/pmc/articles/PMC2921311/.

3. Nicholas A. Christakis, MD, PhD, MPH, and James H. Fowler, PhD, "The Spread of Obesity in a Large Social Network over 32 Years," *New England Journal of Medicine* 357, (2007): 370-379, doi: 10.1056/NEJMsa066082.

4. Jessica J. Chianga, Eisenbergera, Naomi I., Seemanb, Teresa E. and Taylora, Shelley E., "Negative and competitive social interactions are related to heightened proinflammatory cytokine activity," *Proceedings of the National Academy of Sciences in the United States of America* 109, no. 6 (2012): 1878-1882, doi: 10.1073/pnas.1120972109.

CHAPTER SIX

1. Salvador Minuchin, *Families and Family Therapy* (Cambridge, MA: Harvard University Press, 1974).

2. Arnett, Jeffrey Jensen, PhD and Schwab, Joseph, *The Clark University Poll of Parents of Emerging Adults.* 2013. http://www.clarku.edu/clark-poll-emerging-adults/pdfs/clark-university-poll-parents-emerging-adults.pdf.

3. (Joshua Coleman, pers. comm.)

4. Shona Vann, "I've divorced my parents (and it's breaking my heart)," *Daily Mail.com*, February 2011, http://www.dailymail.co.uk/femail/article-1357417/Ive-divorced-parents-breaking-heart--She-blissfully-happy-childhood-So-40-writer-cut-mother-father.html#ixzz3OGUUYTvG.

5. Lise Funderburg, "Why We Break Up With Our Siblings," *TIME*, December 10, 2000, http://content.time.com/time/magazine/article/0,9171,91424,00.html.

CHAPTER SEVEN

1. Ernest B. Harper and Arthur Duhnam, Eds. *Community Organization in Action.* (New York: Association Press, 1959).

2. Sarah Sentilles, "Breaking up with God," *Huffington Post*.com, June, 20, 2011, http://www.huffingtonpost.com/sarah-sentilles/post_2129_b_880665.html.

3. Pew Research Center, "'Nones' on the Rise," October 9, 2012, http://www.pewforum.org/2012/10/09/nones-on-the-rise/.

4. (Paul Grosswald, pers. comm.)

CHAPTER EIGHT

1. Dennis Dailey, PhD, "Circles of Sexuality," http://www.health.state.mn.us/topics/sexualhealth/circlesofsexuality.pdf.

2. Lisa Diamond, *Sexual Fluidity: Understanding Women's Love and Desire.* (Cambridge, MA: Harvard University Press, 2009).

3. Eric Anthony Grollman. "The Kinsey Scale: It's Purpose and Significance." http://www.kinseyconfidential.org/kinsey-scale-purpose-significance.

4. Human Rights Campaign, "Coming Out in the Workplace, as Transgender," http://www.hrc.org/resources/entry/coming-out-in-the-workplace-as-transgender.

5. Health Communities.com, "Transgender Health & Sex Reassignment Surgery," http://www.healthcommunities.com/transgender-health/surgery.shtml.

6. (Hanne Blank, pers. comm.)

7. Katy Winter, "'You are married to the Lord and your daddy is your boyfriend': Purity balls, in which girls 'gift their virginity' to their fathers until marriage, sweeping America," *Daily Mail.com*, March 2014, http://www.dailymail.co.uk/femail/article-2586036/You-married-Lord-daddy-boyfriend-Purity-Balls-girls-gift-virginity-fathers-marriage-sweep-America.html.

8. Daily Mail Reporter: http://www.dailymail.co.uk/femail/article-2270322/Good-morning-parents-Im-gay-How-teenage-girl-came-mom-dad-homemade-cake-letter-witty-baking-puns.html

CHAPTER NINE

1. Myplan.com, "Happiness Index: 300 Careers With The Highest Job Satisfaction Ratings," http://www.myplan.com/careers/top-ten/highest-job-satisfaction.php.
2. The Conference Board, "Job Satisfaction: 2014 Edition," June 2014, http://www.conference-board.org/publications/publicationdetail.cfm?publicationid=2785.

CHAPTER TEN

1. Timaree Schmit, "Timaree's Body: Why Is My Doctor Always Running Late?" *PhillyNow.com*, December 11, 2014, http://phillynow.com/2014/12/11/timarees-body-why-is-my-doctor-always-running-late/.

CHAPTER ELEVEN

1. Chance Allen, "4 Steps to Winning a Breakup," Thought Catalogue, March 2014, http://thoughtcatalog.com/chance-allen/2014/03/4-steps-to-winning-a-breakup/.
2. Jessica K. Witt and Travis E. Dorsch, "Kicking to bigger uprights: Field goal kicking performance influences perceived size," *Perception* 38, no. 9 (2009): 1328-1340, doi:10.1068/p6325.
3. Scapegoating Society: www.scapegoat.demon.co.uk.

CHAPTER TWELVE

1. The Huffington Post Women, "Dealing with a Breakup: 7 Healthy Ways to Cope with Post-Split Stress," Women, *Huffington Post*, June 2013, http://www.huffingtonpost.com/2013/06/05/dealing-with-a-breakup-7-tips_n_3389381.html.

2. Barbara L. Fredrickson, PhD, *Love 2.0: Creating Happiness and Health in Moments of Connection.* (New York: Hudson Street Press, 2013).

3. Radical Forgiveness, http://www.radicalforgiveness.com/.

4. Saima Noreen, Raynette N. Bierman, and Malcom D. MacLeod, "Forgiving You Is Hard, but Forgetting Seems Easy: Can Forgiveness Facilitate Forgetting?" *Psychological Science* 25, no. 7 (2014):1295-1302, doi: 10.1177/0956797614531602.

Acknowledgments

My deepest heartfelt gratitude to . . .

Everyone at Seal for your patience and trust, especially Laura Mazer for pushing me to find this voice and Stephanie Knapp for leading me on this journey. To all of those who helped in big and little ways—meaning everyone who shared their own experiences and break ups (on Facebook, email and phone), I appreciate your candor, stories, and struggles. Heaps of love to my family, friends, classmates and colleagues—you have always been encouraging and supportive of the many ways I continue to evolve and I am forever grateful. Krissy Eliot for your editing, proofreading, and you over all rock star support. Marcia Baczynski (www.askingforwhatyouwant.com), Kate Bornstein (www.katebornstein.typepad.com), Dr. Joshua Coleman (www.dr joshuacoleman.com), Yvette Bowlin (www.declutterist.com), Paul Grosswald, Hanne Blank and Timaree Schmit (www.sexwithtimaree. com) for your expert advice. To Leslie, Sara, Andy and Lauren for getting me to think about this topic. To Scott Player for your patience, understanding and help in finding the time to write this book while juggling (well, not literally) too many other things—including our infant daughter. To. S. Pirate Pearl for being the best baby a mother could ask for and for taking naps long enough to allow me to write.

About the Author

© Circe Photography

Jamye Waxman, M.Ed holds a graduate degree in sex education from Widener University. She started her professional career as a radio producer in New York City. From there, she launched into the field of human sexuality and relationships—as a sex educator, writer and media personality. She is also a sought-after-speaker and media consultant whose work has appeared in magazines including *Women's Health, Men's Health, Playgirl* and *Zink*. She has appeared as a sexuality and relationship expert on the pages of *Heeb, Forbes, Cosmopolitan, Glamour* and *Self* as well as on television: The Doctors, Playboy TV, MTV and The History Channel.

Jamye is the author of *Getting Off: A Woman's Guide to Masturbation* and the co-author of *Hot Sex: Over 200 Things You Can Try Tonight* as well as the Producer/Director of *101 Positions for Lovers*. She also writes for www.gasm.org.

She is currently completing her PhD in Human Sexuality Education and a degree in Marriage and Family Therapy.

She lives in Northern California and online at www.jamye waxman.com.

SELECTED TITLES FROM SEAL PRESS

Crap Job: How to Make the Most of the Job You Hate, by Michelle Goodman. $15.00, 978-1-58005-553-6. Author Michelle Goodman offers practical advice, creative coping strategies, and much-needed comic relief for surviving the workday for the unhappily employed.

Snap Strategies for Couples: 40 Fast Fixes for Everyday Relationship Pitfalls, by Dr. Lana Staheli and Dr. Pepper Schwartz. $16.00, 978-1-58005-562-8. Snap Strategies for Couples offers 40 practical, immediate fixes (or "snaps") for common problems that partners can use to end the fighting, leave the baggage behind, and move their relationships forward.

The New I Do: Reshaping Marriage for Skeptics, Realists and Rebels, by Susan Pease Gadoua and Vicki Larson. $17.00, 978-1-58005-545-1. A new perspective on the modern shape of marriage, this guide offers couples a roadmap for creating alternative marital partnerships.

Break Free from the Divortex: Power Through Your Divorce and Launch Your New Life, by Christina Pesoli. $17.00, 978-1-58005-535-2. An easy-to-follow, all-in-one guide to navigating the perils of divorce and returning to solid emotional ground.

What You Can When You Can: Healthy Living on Your Terms, by Roni Noone and Carla Birnberg. $14.00, 978-1-58005-573-4. This companion book to the #wycwyc movement teaches you how to harness the power of small steps to achieve your goals for healthier living.

Better than Perfect: 7 Strategies to Crush Your Inner Critic and Create a Life You Love, by Elizabeth Lombardo. $17.00, 978-1-58005-549-9. A proven, powerful method for shaking the chains of perfectionism and finding balance in life.

FIND SEAL PRESS ONLINE
www.sealpress.com
www.facebook.com/sealpress
Twitter: @SealPress